The College of Charleston
Charleston, South Carolina

Written by Melanie Murray
Edited by Adam Fleming, Matt Ornowski

Additional contributions by Omid Gohari,
Christina Koshzow, Adam Burns, Chris Mason, Joey Rahimi,
Jon Skindzier, Luke Skurman, Tim Williams
James Balzer and Kristen Burns

ISBN # 1-59658-029-1
ISSN # 1551-9740
© Copyright 2005 College Prowler
All Rights Reserved
Printed in the U.S.A.
www.collegeprowler.com

Special thanks to Babs Carryer, Andy Hannah, LaunchCyte, Tim O'Brien, Bob Sehlinger, Thomas Emerson, Andrew Skurman, Barbara Skurman, Bert Mann, Dave Lehman, Daniel Fayock, Chris Babyak, The Donald H. Jones Center for Entrepreneurship, Terry Slease, Jerry McGinnis, Bill Ecenberger, Idie McGinty, Kyle Russell, Jacque Zaremba, Larry Winderbaum, Paul Kelly, Roland Allen, Jon Reider, Team Evankovich, Julie Fenstermaker, Lauren Varacalli, Abu Noaman, Jason Putorti, Mark Exler, Daniel Steinmeyer, Jared Cohon, Gabriela Oates, Tri Ad Litho, David Koegler, Glen Meakem, and the **College of Charleston Bounce Back Team.**

College Prowler™
5001 Baum Blvd.
Suite 456
Pittsburgh, PA 15213

Phone: (412) 697-1390, 1(800) 229-4675
Fax: (412) 697-1396, 1(800) 772-4972
E-mail: info@collegeprowler.com
Website: www.collegeprowler.com

Welcome to College Prowler™

During the writing of College Prowler's guidebooks, we felt it was critical that our content was unbiased and unaffiliated with any college or university. We think it's important that our readers get honest information and a realistic impression of the student opinions on any campus — that's why if any aspect of a particular school is terrible, we (unlike a campus brochure) intend to publish it. While we do keep an eye out for the occasional extremist — the cheerleader or the cynic — we take pride in letting the students tell it like it is. We strive to create a book that's as representative as possible of each particular campus. Our books cover both the good and the bad, and whether the survey responses point to recurring trends or a variation in opinion, these sentiments are directly and proportionally expressed through our guides.

College Prowler guidebooks are in the hands of students throughout the entire process of their creation. Because you can't make student-written guides without the students, we have students at each campus who help write, randomly survey their peers, edit, layout, and perform accuracy checks on every book that we publish. From the very beginning, student writers gather the most up-to-date stats, facts, and inside information on their colleges. They fill each section with student quotes and summarize the findings in editorial reviews. In addition, each school receives a collection of letter grades (A through F) that reflect student opinion and help to represent contentment, prominence, or satisfaction for each of our 20 specific categories. Just as in grade school, the higher the mark the more content, more prominent, or more satisfied the students are with the particular category.

Once a book is written, additional students serve as editors and check for accuracy even more extensively. Our bounce-back team — a group of randomly selected students who have no involvement with the project — are asked to read over the material in order to help ensure that the book accurately expresses every aspect of the university and its students. This same process is applied to the 200-plus schools College Prowler currently covers. Each book is the result of endless student contributions, hundreds of pages of research and writing, and countless hours of hard work. All of this has led to the creation of a student information network that stretches across the nation to every school that we cover. It's no easy accomplishment, but it's the reason that our guides are such a great resource.

When reading our books and looking at our grades, keep in mind that every college is different and that the students who make up each school are not uniform — as a result, it is important to assess schools on a case-by-case basis. Because it's impossible to summarize an entire school with a single number or description, each book provides a dialogue, not a decision, that's made up of 20 different topics and hundreds of student quotes. In the end, we hope that this guide will serve as a valuable tool in your college selection process. Enjoy!

OMID GOHARI ○ CHRISTINA KOSHZOW ○ CHRIS MASON ○ JOEY RAHIMI ○ LUKE SKURMAN ○

Founders of College Prowler™

Table of Contents

Introduction from the Author

Greetings students, current and future. You may have never heard of the College of Charleston, though it's a historic landmark both in the state of South Carolina and in the United States. It's the oldest municipal college in the country, and has grown from a founding class of twenty-three to a student population of over ten thousand. This may not mean much to you, and I can honestly say that when I was contemplating my academic future, it didn't have much sway over my decision either. But these facts are some of many that make attending C of C a rewarding and valuable experience. Not many schools possess the history or environment that can be found at the College of Charleston, and not many schools ever will. But more importantly, you can be sure that here at C of C, you're in good hands, and so is your future. Here, you'll not graduate empty-handed.

The professors and faculty here genuinely care about the academic welfare of their students, and want nothing more than to open more avenues for fruitful and rewarding futures, whether it is a career, or a continuation of your higher education. There are many reasons to attend C of C, and many of them are detailed in this guidebook. But don't get me wrong. the College of Charleston is not for everyone, and this book is not designed to be propaganda. It is simply here to inform you of what is offered at the College of Charleston, and to hopefully help guide you to the school that is right for you. With this guidebook, you can make a more informed decision about what you like and dislike about the College of Charleston, and investigate further what you are really looking for in a college or university. This book is here to help you in any way it can, and I hope it does, wherever you end up in your pursuit of higher learning.

Sincerely yours,
Melanie Murray

By the Numbers

General Information

College of Charleston
66 George St.
Charleston, South Carolina
29424

Control:
Public

Academic Calendar:
Semester

Religious Affiliation:
None

Founded:
1770

Website:
http://www.cofc.edu

Main Phone:
(843) 953-5507

Admissions Phone:
(843) 953-5670

Student Body

Full-Time Undergraduates:
8,921

Part-Time Undergraduates:
903

Male Undergraduates:
3,627 (37%)

Female Undergraduates:
6,197 (63%)

Admissions

Overall Acceptance Rate:
60%

Regular Decision Acceptance Rate:
57%

Total Applicants:
7,606

Total Acceptances:
4,560

Freshman Enrollment:
1,874

Yield (% of admitted students who actually enroll):
41%

Transfer Applications Received:
2,074

Transfer Applications Accepted:
1,306

Transfer Students Enrolled:
629

Transfer Student Yield:
48%

Early Decision Available?
No

Early Action Available?
Yes

Regular Decision Deadline:
April 1

Regular Decision Notification:
April 15

Must-Reply-By Date:
May 1

Common Application Accepted?
Yes

Supplemental Forms?
Yes

Admissions Phone:
(843) 953-5670

Admissions E-mail:
Admissions@cofc.edu

Admissions Website:
www.cofc.edu/admissions

SAT I or ACT Required?
Either

**SAT I Range
(25th – 75th Percentile):**
1120-1280

**SAT I Verbal Range
(25th – 75th Percentile):**
560-640

**SAT I Math Range
(25th – 75th Percentile):**
560-640

Retention Rate:
70%

**Top 10% of
High School Class:**
28%

Application Fee:
$35 Online, $45 Paper

Financial Information

Tuition:
$6,202 (In-state)
$14,140 (Out-of-state)

Room and Board:
$6,506

Books and Supplies for class:
Ranges from $100 to $800.

**Average Need-Based
Financial Aid Package:**
$8,698

**Students Who
Applied For Financial Aid:**
51%

Students Who Received Aid:
38%

Financial Aid Forms Deadline:
March 1

Financial Aid Phone:
(843) 953-5540

Financial Aid E-mail:
financialaid@cofc.edu

Financial Aid Website:
http://www.cofc.edu/finaid

Academics

The Lowdown On...
Academics

Degrees Awarded:
Bachelor's, Master's,
Post-Bachelor Certification

Most Popular Areas of Study:

Communications 18%

Business 14%

Psychology 8%

Biology 7%

Elementary Education 7%

Undergraduate Schools:

School of the Arts

School of Economics

School of Education

School of Humanities and Social Sciences

School of Science and Mathematics

Four Year Graduation Rate:
36%

Five Year Graduation Rate:
53%

Six Year Graduation Rate:
55%

Full-Time Faculty:
487

Part-Time Faculty:
366

Faculty with Terminal Degree:
85.6%

Student-to-Faculty Ratio:
14:1

Average Course Load:
15 credits

Special Degree Options

Charleston offers various interdisciplinary majors, in addition to a couple of pre-professional programs (pre-medicine and pre-dentistry) and teacher certification.

AP Test Score Requirements

Possible credit for scores of 3

IB Test Score Requirements

Possible credit for scores of 5, 6 or 7

Academic Clubs

Biology Club, Arabic Club, Marketing Club, Visual Arts Club, Golden Key Honor Society, PETE (Physical Education Teacher Education), Historic Preservation Alliance, American Student Dental Association, Honors Program Student Association, MESSA (Master of Environmental Studies Student Association)

Did You Know?

- **Charleston graduation** occurs on Mother's Day every year and instead of caps and gowns, the girls wear white dresses and the guys wear tuxes. Not too shabby.

- Charleston's campus, as well as being scenic and beautiful, is full of places for **outdoor studying,** like the lawn in front of Randolph Hall, or the center of campus near the Physician's Auditorium.

- During final and midterm exams, Craig Cafeteria plays host to a **midnight breakfast,** so students can take a break, grab a bite to eat, and relax away some stress during cram-time.

- The College of Charleston's **On Course program** is a flexible, easy-to-use audit processing program that makes it faster and easier for students to keep up with their degree, credits, scheduling and GPA.

Best Places to Study

- Students looking for **peace and quiet** should head to the library or either the third or fourth floor of the Stern Center.

Students Speak Out On...
Academics

"English teachers here are awesome. I haven't met one in the three years I've been here that hasn't changed the way I view my major. They really want you to absorb as much information as you can while you're here."

Q "**It's impossible to make a general statement about the faculty here.** Some are awesome and you want to take their classes over and over again, but others are plain and simple, not good professors."

Q "I really thought I would hate my biology professor, just because I hate biology and I was biased. But I couldn't really hate them. They know that **a lot of their students don't really want to be there,** and that some need extra help. They really do want you to pass their class even if you have to do it kicking and screaming."

Q "I don't think that the College of Charleston is negligent in their responsibility to hire professors who are capable in their field, but sometimes professors are just unfair — not giving enough warning before assignments, changing due dates, testing on things that weren't discussed in class, stuff like that. **Some professors just suck,** but I guess that happens at every college."

Q "The College is **really devoted to the success of its students.** The professors know you by name, and they are always available. There are programs here to help you if you're struggling. There's never a time when you can't find help."

Q "This school is not easy, but I've learned that if you **get help from your advisor** and know what classes you're getting yourself into, you should never find yourself in a situation that's impossible to get out of."

Q "The language department seems to be the worst one in the whole college. The professors I experienced there were the meanest and strictest, but others seemed to also be the most **unqualified and ineffective.** There was no medium between professors who didn't know what they were doing and professors who acted like, well, not nice."

Q "I have to say **I was a little disappointed by the variety of classes** provided here. There should be more classes for film and writing, and they shouldn't be electives. I mean, this is a liberal arts college, right?"

Q "There will always be **professors that can taint your impression** of the faculty here. But you can't say that you haven't really enjoyed, if not loved, the reigning majority of your courses here."

Q **"The faculty is nice.** I heard that the dean let a student park her car in his driveway for a week when she couldn't afford to pay for the student garage."

Q "I love the theater department here. The way you talk to other students is the way you talk to your professors. **They really want to inspire you,** whether you're in Intro to Theater or a theater major, they want you to love theater."

Q "I really feel like the professors here, for the most part, treat their students like equals. I've had a couple professors who insisted on being called by their first names. That **really takes the pressure off."**

Q "It's normal in college to skip a few classes, or even a lot of classes. But I've learned from my own personal experience, that **teachers test on lecture material** and hardly ever open the book. So skipping classes too much is pretty much the stupidest thing you could do at this school."

Q "At first I was wondering about the quality of education here, but since I've declared my major, **I've gotten so many opportunities** and so much encouragement that I know I wouldn't get anywhere else."

The College Prowler Take On...
Academics

One thing can be said about the College of Charleston: students will experience a range of emotions when it comes to their professors. This is true no matter where you go, but what makes the College of Charleston unique is the relationship between professors and students. With a student-to-teacher ratio of fourteen to one, you can always be certain that availability and attention will be provided in abundance. The vast majority of students at Charleston feel that their professors view them as equals and sincerely care about how they are doing in class, whether it's an advanced English class or an elective film studies. The SNAP (Students Needing Access Parity) program is a perfect example of this. Students with disabilities receive assistance in meeting with their professors. Probably the biggest issue facing Charleston academics at the moment is General Education requirements. In order to graduate, students must fulfill these requirements, which, coupled with a student's major requirements (most of which involve writing a Senior Thesis) can be very difficult for a student to complete. Compounding the problem is the fact that entry level Natural Science courses are almost always over-packed, some by as many as one hundred students. The system may have a few flaws, but the professors and the courses offered are above average to say the least. So, for Pete's sake, let them get a good night's sleep.

The College Prowler™ Grade on
Academics: B-

A high Academics grade generally indicates that professors are knowledgeable, accessible, and genuinely interested in their students' welfare. Other determining factors include class size, how well professors communicate, and whether or not classes are engaging.

Local Atmosphere

The Lowdown On...
Local Atmosphere

Region:
Southeast

City, State:
Charleston, South Carolina

Setting:
Medium-sized city

Distance from Columbia (state capitol):
115 Miles

Distance from Myrtle Beach:
98 Miles

→

Points of Interest:

Market Street

Spoleto Arts Festival

Charleston Ghost and Dungeon Tour

Civil War Walk

South Carolina Aquarium

Patriots' Point Naval and Maritime Museum

Historical Old Exchange and Provost Dungeon

Waterfront Park

Dock Street Theater

The Hunley Submarine

The Charleston Symphony Orchestra.

Closest Shopping Malls:

Shops at King Street, Citadel Mall, Village Square Shopping Center, Mount Pleasant Towne Center.

Closest Movie Theatres:

AMC Citadel Mall
2072 Sam Rittenburg Blvd.
Charleston, SC, 29407
Phone: (843) 763-7052

America Cinema Grill
446 King St.
Charleston, SC, 29403
Phone: (843) 722-3456

Eastern Federal Movies at Mount Pleasant
963 Houston-Northcutt Blvd.
Mount Pleasant, SC, 29464
Phone: (843) 884-4900

Major Sports Teams:

Charleston Battery (soccer), Charleston Stingrays (hockey), Charleston Riverdogs (minor league baseball).

City Websites

http://www.charleston.cvb.com

http://www.ci.charleston.sc.us

http://www.charleston.com

Did You Know?

Charleston, South Carolina's oldest city, has a **sixteenth place** ranking out of twenty cites for the best quality of life in the nation, according to easidemographics.com.

Five Fun Facts about Charleston:

- The College of Charleston is the **oldest city-run college** in the United States, and one of the five oldest colleges in the country.

- "Gone with the Wind," "White Squall," "The Patriot" (with Mel Gibson, not Steven Seagal), "O," "Cold Mountain," and many other movies were **filmed in Charleston.**

- Just take if from Scarlett O'Hara: Charleston tops the list of **best-mannered cities** in the United States for the ninth consecutive year.

- Every year the city of Charleston rakes in **over 4 billion dollars** from over 5 million tourists.

- The **Spoleto Arts Festival,** which is held every spring in Charleston and lasts two and a half weeks, is the most comprehensive arts festival in the country.

Famous Charlestonians:

Dubose Heyward, author of "Porgy," later adapted into the famous musical "Porgy and Bess" by George Gershwin, **Padgett Powell,** author of "Edisto" and "Aliens of Affection," **Andy Dick,** comedian and actor

Local Atmosphere

> "I love Charleston because we're in an urban setting, but it's not a big city that overwhelms you. The beach is twenty minutes in practically every direction, and so are the suburbs. There are so many places to go, but why would you want to go anywhere else? It's Charleston!"

Q "It's nice having other schools nearby, like Charleston Southern University and the Citadel. **You can always get away from the city** and hang out on a different campus if you need to."

Q "I love Charleston's location! It's not like a normal campus. It's right in the middle of the city, so **you can walk anywhere you need to go.**"

Q **"The history here is so rich.** Sure, not a lot of celebrities are from here, or come here to visit, but I've seen a few. Everything is so old and authentic, and we get the privilege of living in it every day. Everywhere you go, there's an interesting story."

Q "It's hard with all the tourists sometimes. Charleston isn't that big to begin with, and when huge buses clog the streets, it's pretty annoying. But **it's cool that our home is interesting and beautiful** enough to draw that much attention."

Q "Sometimes **it's a little overwhelming to live in the city** when you're from a small town. I know some people who have transferred because they didn't feel right here. There are so many people from small towns here! Imagine what they would do in New York City!"

Q "I'm from Atlanta, and this city seems kind of small and quaint in comparison. But **it's peaceful and quiet**. You can still get crazy though, don't get me wrong. It's fun. It's just not big."

The College Prowler Take On...
Local Atmosphere

Charleston is a city preserved by care and untainted by change and novelty. This isn't to say that Charleston is outdated or boring. Aside from being a beautiful and historic city, Charleston offers a variety of activities and events to choose from. Two other colleges, CSU and the Citadel are nearby, so even though Charleston is not a huge college town, there are enough college students to go around. Whether you're into sports or art, outdoor activities or indoor, shopping or surfing, there is always something to do. Shops on King and Meeting Streets are only blocks away from campus. Beaches (yes, more than one) are only a twenty minute drive. And there are more restaurants downtown than anyone could ever eat at in a lifetime.

You will not hear many stories of Hollywood celebrities graduating from the College or building a summer home here, but there are many other stories to tell that are rich in history, meaning and significance. Even students who have come to know Charleston as their home are freshly impressed and amazed by the beauty and history this city has to offer. The vendors on Market Street are popular among students and tourists alike. Even just taking a leisurely walk around town is sure to be a feast for the eyes. If you are looking for skyscrapers, rush-hour traffic and the hustle and bustle of a metropolis, search elsewhere. But if you are looking for laid-back, easy-going Southern culture, Charleston is just right for you.

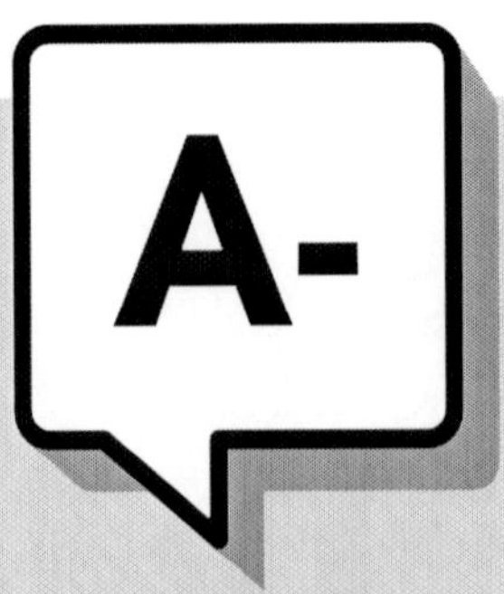

The College Prowler™ Grade on

Local Atmosphere: A-

A high Local Atmosphere grade indicates that the area surrounding campus is safe and scenic. Other factors include nearby attractions, proximity to other schools, and the town's attitude toward students

Safety & Security

The Lowdown On...
Safety & Security

Number of C of C Police:

36 trained police officers, 15 security guards assigned to residence halls

Phone:

(843) 953-5611

Safety Services:

Bicycle Registration

Campus Emergency Call Boxes

C.A.R.E (Crisis Assistance Response and Education)

First Responder Unit

Parking Enforcement

RAD (Rape Aggression Defense)

Health Services:
Confidential Care
Minor Injuries/Sickness
Gynecological Care
STD Testing
Immunization Updates
Tuberculosis Skin Testing
Asthma Care
Allergy Shots
Assistance with Referrals
Respiratory and
Dermatological Care
Diagnostic Testing

Student Health Services:
College of Charleston
181 Calhoun St.
Charleston, SC 29424

Health Center Office Hours
Monday-Thursday 8:30 a.m.-7 p.m.; Friday: 8:30 a.m.-5 p.m.

Website: http://www.wellness.cofc.edu/health.htm

> **"The campus police here always seem to be watching you, but that means they're watching the shady people, too, which makes me feel more comfortable."**

Q "The police on campus do a really good job, even though sometimes they can be jerks. But they're just doing their jobs, I guess. **They make me feel safe**, so they must be doing something right."

Q "Obviously, since the college is located downtown, **there are going to be crimes and incidents** that public safety can't always stop. But when I am on campus, I know that public safety [officers] are the ones around the street corner at night, not a mugger."

Q **"They piss me off sometimes**, like when they check everything in your bag if you're going into the dorm at night. But I've heard some really horrible stories of what happens at other schools when security was lax. And if someone has a gun or a bomb in their bag, I'd rather have public safety enforcing all the rules instead of letting any psycho stroll by."

Q "The only thing that annoys me about public safety is how strict they are with alcohol in the dorms. Before I got here, **I heard that ten people got kicked out of the dorms at once** after their first strike with alcohol. That scared me. But obviously people are still getting it into the dorms, and they always will. If you can't get it into the dorm, it's really not that big a deal, just drink it somewhere else."

Q "It's not like we have fat, slow, lazy security guards 'protecting' us. **They're real cops**, and they have real guns, and as bad as that sounds, I feel safer around an officer with a gun than a security guard without one."

Q "Public safety has taught me to never throw a keg party at my house. If they break it up, **they could fine you over a thousand dollars** for noise violation. No thanks."

Q "Because our school is in the city, **public safety is like, doubly careful.** They keep students as safe as they can. I guess it's the city police that's to blame for the college kids that get mugged walking home late at night."

Q "They're everywhere! You can't stand on the street corner with a beer in your hand without getting caught! But **they're pretty cool about letting people leave parties** even though they know they've been drinking."

Q **"My bike has been stolen twice.** You're telling me public safety is doing a good job and they can't even keep people's bikes from being stolen?"

Q "I like the fact that we have emergency call boxes on campus. **You can call a public safety officer any time** — day or night — and they'll take you wherever you want to go, even if you just have a bad feeling about the street or something. That makes me feel safe on campus."

Statistics show that the College of Charleston, even with its urban setting, is no more dangerous than a college or university with a closed campus. Thirty six professionally trained police officers (a large number in comparison to other colleges much larger than the College of Charleston) patrol the campus and surrounding areas twenty four hours a day and fifteen security officers are stationed in the residence halls. Sometimes students feel that campus security is more like campus surveillance; police officers are on just about every corner, they even check your bags when you enter the residence halls after a certain hour of night. And just because the guards at the dorms are not police officers doesn't mean security in the dorms is lax. Every dorm has a different colored sticker that residents must have on their student ID's. Without this sticker, you can't get in except as a guest, and every guest's information is taken down by the guard at the front desk. Overall, students feel that security officers are doing a good job (in spite of occasional bike thefts here and there). Incidents of violence and crime are nearly unheard of on the college's campus, though. Most cases of burglary, vandalism and assault (aside from confrontations and fights) occur outside the boundaries of campus because, in large part, of the efforts of public safety working to secure university grounds. Obviously, it's a student's responsibility to take care of themselves and their property on and off campus, but when they can't, or a threat seems to be present, public safety is always there to do what they can.

The College Prowler™ Grade on

Safety & Security: B

A high grade in Safety & Security means that students generally feel safe, campus police are visible, blue-light phones and escort services are readily available, and safety precautions are not overly necessary.

Computers

The Lowdown On...
Computers

High-Speed Network?
Yes

Number of Labs:
16

Wireless Network?
Yes

Operating Systems:
Mac
PC

24-Hour Labs

No

Charge to Print?

Printing is free in the library computer lab, but it costs 10 cents a page everywhere else.

Did You Know?

- Charleston features both **Computer Classrooms and Smart Classrooms.** A Computer Classroom contains a PC for each student and an LCD projector for the professor. A Smart Classroom contains only the projector and one computer for the professor.

Computers

> **"Most students you ask here won't know that much about computers. We use them when we need them for school and a couple other things. We're not experts around here."**

Q "You don't have to have your own computer here. I've seen kids who have gotten by without one. But I went a semester without a working computer and it was hell. **It's best to have one."**

Q **"You don't have to have a laptop. T**here aren't students all over the place clicking away on their computers. I haven't seen even five people sitting around in between classes with their laptops. A regular desktop will do."

Q "The library is a good place to go if you have no computer or even if you do, to find some peace and quiet. **The lab is only full in the library during exams** and stuff. But printing is free."

Q "The computer lab in the library is okay, but it sucks during exam time. **Even at four in the morning you can't get on a computer.** But most of the year, the computer labs are always available. And with a new library, things can only get better."

Q "I don't know anything about computers, and **I've gotten by fine here when I've had computer problems.** One of your friends is bound to know how to fix something if you're completely stumped."

Q "Don't call campus technologies. I had a problem with my Mac, and when the person got here to fix it he was like 'Oops! I don't do Macs. I only do PCs.' Give me a break. **They're idiots, and you have to pay them.**"

Q "If you don't want to go to the library to work, **you can always go to a departmental lab.** They're everywhere, and the people there are just as helpful."

Q **"I've seen a lot of viruses on our network here.** I've gotten two viruses so far at this school. Be careful about what e-mails you open. The school's network somehow makes it easier for people to contaminate lots of people at one time."

Q "I love my computer. With classes that assign twenty-page term papers, **it's good to have your own computer,** because it's one thing to work your butt off for a class, but to spend all your time in the library working your butt off? No thanks."

The College Prowler Take On...
Computers

The administration realizes that in order to be competitive, students must have access to the latest technologies. C of C is constantly updating their computer systems and network servers, not only for security purposes, but also to provide its student body with the most up-to-date computing available and the quickest network speed possible. This includes Ethernet connections and wired classrooms, along with a wireless network available at various locations. Many instructors now use C of C's Blackboard system to post class notes, assignments, and grades that are easy for students to access from any computer location, regardless if you own one or not.

Some students complain about crowded computer labs or occasional viruses that prevent them from doing schoolwork, but these are usually the ones who wait until the last minute to complete their assignments. Also, the school has adopted a more strict policy on file trading due to the strain it puts on the network servers and to avoid the possibility of copyright infringement lawsuits. This new enforcement helps to speed up the network. In addition to these new policies, the systems have been upgraded as well, continuing to make the network quicker. Having your own computer is not a necessity at C of C, but it's nice to have the convenience of checking your e-mail or communicating via instant messenger in the comfort of your room.

The College Prowler™ Grade on

Computers: B-

A high grade in Computers designates that computer labs are available, the computer network is easily accessible, and the campus' computing technology is up-to-date.

Facilities

The Lowdown On...
Facilities

Campus Size:
52 Acres

Student Center:
Stern Center on George Street

Athletic Center:
Stern Center

F. Mitchell Johnson Center

Libraries:
The Robert Scott Small Library, the Marine Resources Library, the John Rivers Communications Museum, the Avery Research Center, and the Office of Media and Technology make up the College's library system. The Marlene and Nathan Addlestone Library is new for the Fall 2004 semester.

Bar on Campus?

No

What Is There to Do On Campus?

When not in class, students can use both fitness centers on campus, grab a bite at any of the dining halls, see a play in the Simons Art Center or relax on the Cistern in front of Randolph Hall, all without ever leaving campus.

Movie Theatre on Campus?

Movies are shown twice a month in the Sotille Theater on George Street and in the Education Center.

Coffeehouse on Campus?

Yes, at the Port City Java in the Stern Center. Also there is a Starbuck's and another Port City Java less than a block away from campus.

Favorite Things to do?

The center of campus, in between Maybank Hall and the Robert S. Small Library, is a popular place for students to hang out in between classes, and tables are usually set up by campus organizations such as Greek Life and the athletic teams. Napping on the lawn in front of Randolph Hall is always a popular activity. The Stern Center Gardens plays host to live music functions. Several buildings on campus hold poetry readings, lectures, debates, and films.

Students Speak Out On...
Facilities

"Sometimes the bathrooms make me feel like I'm in high school again. But that's just because they're kind of old. They're clean, and I'm not afraid to go into them or anything."

Q **"I'm glad they built a new fitness center.** The first one was always so crowded. You could never find a machine when you needed one. But now that there are two, you don't have to worry about finding equipment."

Q "I love the arena. The energy during a game is so high; **you can't help but enjoy yourself,** even if you're there only for social reasons."

Q **"They show movies a couple times a month** at the Sotille, and they're brand new too. There are always packs of kids walking down George Street to go see whatever they're showing."

Q "Since I've been here, they've built a new dorm, a new garage, remodeled the Stern Center, remodeled Barry Hall, and put in a new diner. And now **they're building a brand new library.** I love how they are always trying to make things newer and better for us."

Q "I don't really have much to do with the athletic places. But I like that they offer **yoga and dance classes** for free."

Q "If you're not on an athletic team, the facilities here can be frustrating. **The pool hours for general use are ridiculous** and unless you're on the team, you can hardly ever use it."

The College Prowler Take On...
Facilities

Students feel that for the most part, the amount of facilities provided by the College of Charleston is suitable, and the school is making further attempts to accommodate its students. Newly built residence halls will allow housing for the growing influx of students. The newly remodeled Joe E. Barry Hall shows that the College doesn't neglect its older buildings. Also newly remodeled, the student center can now hold more people and provide more helpful services. The Stern Center, which is the best-equipped building for student needs, houses meeting rooms, a food court, a swimming pool, and a large ballroom for various events. There's also a second fitness center, much to the joy of students who have had to wait their turn to in line to work out. While most students are satisfied with campus facilities, some students are disappointed with the bathrooms (you can't please everyone). Sometimes it may seem that the College of Charleston has tried to cram too many things into a small amount of space. The Stern Center with its many facilities is an example of this; if there were only one building that could be considered the "central" building on campus, this would be it. The arts center is spacious and includes a courtyard that can be enjoyed by all students, not just artists. With the exception of relatively new buildings (new meaning built within the last 100 years), the facilities that have stood in the city of Charleston for over 200 years are the ones used by the College. Even on campus, where the city has seen the most architectural change, the sights are pleasing to the eye.

The College Prowler™ Grade on

Facilities: B

A high Facilities grade indicates that the campus is aesthetically pleasing and well-maintained; facilities are state-of-the-art, and libraries are exceptional. Other determining factors include the quality of both athletic and student centers and an abundance of things to do on campus.

Campus Dining

The Lowdown On...
Campus Dining

Freshman Meal Plan Requirement?
Yes

Meal Plan Average Cost:
Between $360 and $1030

Places to Grab a Bite with Your Meal Plan:

Cornerstone Bistro

Location: McAlister Residence Hall

Food: Sandwiches, Salads, Soups

Hours: Monday-Thursday 8 a.m.-12 a.m.; Friday 8 a.m.-10 p.m.; Saturday 11 a.m.- 8 p.m.; Sunday 11 a.m.-12 a.m.

You can use your Dining Dollars to enjoy the Bistro's sandwiches, fresh make-your-own salad bar, and smoothies. The Bistro is the trendy place to eat on campus.

Craig Café

Location: Craig Residence Hall

Food: Variety

Hours: Breakfast: Monday-Friday 7:15 a.m.-10 a.m., Saturday-Sunday 8:30 a.m.-10 a.m.; Lunch: Monday-Friday 11 a.m.-2:30 p.m., Saturday-Sunday 11 a.m.-2 p.m.; Dinner: Monday-Thursday 4 p.m.-8 p.m., Friday-Sunday 4 p.m.-7 p.m.

Come to Craig Café for home style meals, Italian dishes like pasta casseroles and calzones, grilled sandwiches, and a fresh salad bar. This eatery offers many choices, so you're sure to find something you like.

Danforth Dining Center

Location: Susan B. Anthony

Food: All buffet style, all-you-can-eat, varying foods

Favorite dish: Chinese stir-fry

Hours: Mon- Fri. 4:30 p.m.-8 p.m., Sat., Sun. 9:00- 2 p.m., 4:30 p.m.-8 p.m.

Douglass Dining Center

Location: Douglass

Food: Wraps, quesadillas, "home-cooked" food, soups

Favorite dish: Chicken and cheese quesadilla

Hours: Mon- Fri 10 a.m.- 8 p.m.

Hillside Café

Location: Susan B. Anthony

Food: Pizza, desserts, sandwiches, coffee drinks, smoothies

Favorite Food: StrawBarry yogurt smoothie

Hours: Mon. – Sun. 12 p.m. – 1 a.m., Closed, Mon- Fri 4:30-8:30

Hungry Cougar

Location: Joe E. Barry Residence Hall

Food: Variety

Hours: Monday-Thursday 7 a.m.-10 p.m.; Friday 7 a.m.-8 p.m.; Saturday 11 a.m.-8 p.m.; Sunday 11 a.m.-10 p.m.

Hungry Cougar has four stations: HomeZone, Montague's Deli, Bené Pizza & Pasta, and Grab & Go. You have your choice of home style dishes, sandwiches, salads, pizza, and even sushi. Students can use either their café meals or their Dining Dollars to purchase meals.

The Meliora

Location: Above Douglass Dining Center

Food: Sit-down with sandwiches, soup. entrees, desserts

Favorite food: Grilled cheese

Hours: Mon-Fri. 11:30 a.m.- 2 p.m.

The Stern Center Food Court

Location: The Stern Center

Food: Fast Food

Hours: Monday-Thursday 7 a.m.-10 p.m.; Friday 7 a.m.- 8 p.m.; Saturday 11 a.m.- 8 p.m.; Sunday 11 a.m.- 10 p.m.

The Stern Center's food court has fast food favorites such as Chik-Fil-A, Burger King, Asian Express, and Java City. It's a great place to meet up with friends for a quick meal, snack, dessert, or cup of coffee. Use your Dining Dollars to eat here.

Places Off-Campus To Use Your Champ Card:

East Bay Deli

Food: Sandwiches, Soups

Address: 334 East Bay St.

Phone: (843) 723-1234

Hours: Monday-Friday 8:30 a.m.-9 p.m.

A great place for lunch, you can come here for soups, a fresh salad bar, wraps and other sandwiches for an alternative to campus sandwiches.

Groucho's Deli

http://www.grouchos.com
Food: Sandwiches
364 King St.
Charleston, SC 29401
Phone: (843) 534-1436
Hours: Monday-Saturday 11 a.m.-8:30 p.m.; Sunday 11 a.m.-4 p.m.
Groucho's serves up a lot of original soups and sandwiches and offers plenty of specialties.

Joe Pasta

Food: Italian

Address: 433 King St.

Phone: (843) 965-5252

Hours: Sunday-Thursday 11:30 a.m.-10 p.m.; Friday-.Saturday 11:30 a.m.-12 a.m.

Joe Pasta is a popular Italian restaurant in the historic area of downtown Charleston. Use your Champ Card here and make a lunch or dinner out of a variety of pastas and other Italian favorites.

The Kickin' Chicken

Food: Sandwiches, Salads

Address: 337 King St.

Charleston, SC 29401

Phone: (843) 805-5020

The Kickin' Chicken has some of the best chicken sandwiches around and also serves up salads and pitas. If you're not hungry, you can still come here for the nightlife as the restaurant is also a venue for local bands to perform.

Moe's Southwest Grill

http://www.moes.com

Food: Tex-Mex

Address: 381 King St.

Phone: (843) 577-7720

Moe's has a variety of tacos, burritos, quesadillas and other Mexican favorites. Want Mexican and meatless, too? You can substitute tofu for meat in several of Moe's menu items.

Student Favorites

Kickin' Chicken

Moe's

24-Hour
On-Campus Eating?

No

Other Options:

There is a kosher deli as part of Douglass Dining Center or Uncle Dicky's parks on the Fraternity Quad on the weekends, with the popular favorite cheese fries and other heart-healthy foods.

Did You Know?

• Meal plans at Charleston include **Dining Dollars,** money stored in a student's account that can be used like a credit card at dining halls.

• The College of Charleston meal plan offers another option, called the **Champ Card,** which allows students to dine at various Charleston restaurants on a pre-paid plan.

Campus Dining

> **"I hate the cafeteria sometimes. When it's cold, it seems so far away. But you can really fill up there, and there's such a good variety of stuff. Salads there are awesome."**

Q "There's really no reason to get a meal plan after your freshman year. If you get Dining Dollars, you have a lot more options and you can always eat at the cafeteria if you want to. But **you shouldn't limit yourself to just a meal plan."**

Q **"I love the Champ Card!** I can eat out any time I want. But you do have to be careful not to use it too many times too fast. If the Champ Card is all you have, you could find yourself starving and broke at the end of the year."

Q "I hate the HomeZone. If there wasn't a dorm above it I would want someone to burn it down. There is no excuse for our parents paying the money they pay for the crap they call food in the HomeZone. **It makes me sick just looking at it** sometimes."

Q "I don't know why, but **I kind of like the cafeteria.** Considering the fact that I can't really afford to eat out whenever I want, it's pretty good for the bare minimum."

Q "There could definitely be more places to eat on campus, and the food in the Hungry Cougar is just plain pathetic for the most part. The food there **reminds me of what I ate in my high school cafeteria**, only then I wasn't paying for it."

Q "There are so many restaurants outside of campus that being a poor college student hurts even more when you're starving and you can't eat what you want. But **the meal plan has so many different options;** you can pre-pay for all your meals and never once have to eat at the cafeteria."

Q **"Dining Dollars can run out very quickly,** I've learned. Especially if you go to Barry to get some food and you take a look at what they're serving in the HomeZone. You'll most likely always pick pizza or sushi instead."

Q "Our cafeteria is OK, but we need more places to eat where you can use a meal plan. I like the Bistro because it's right under my dorm, and **I can always run down and get a snack."**

Q "The Bistro is a **good place to hang out and chill between classes** and grab a bite to eat. It's a lot more convenient than going to the cafeteria and standing in line for a whole meal."

Q "The cafeteria seems to be a pretty popular place. **At lunchtime it's packed**, and it's not all freshmen, so the food can't be that bad."

Q "I think the Champ Card is a rip-off. You're not getting a deal, or getting free meals. **You're paying for every scrap of food you eat**, just all at once instead of in increments. Don't be fooled. It's a good arrangement, but it's not like the College is getting shafted."

Q **"Never get just a meal plan.** You're completely
stuck when all your friends want to go to Joe Pasta or
something and you have to go to the cafeteria. Part of
being in Charleston is experiencing the food. Definitely
get a Champ Card or Dining Dollars."

Q "I've only been here for one year and I have a meal plan.
But I will probably get one next year too, just because
it's the easiest thing, and you get **the most food for the
least amount of money."**

The College Prowler Take On...
Campus Dining

There will always be mixed emotions when it comes to campus dining, but every student can pretty much agree that the dining hall leaves much to be desired. Though the food at the HomeZone may be nearly inedible by students' standards, the quality of the food in Craig Café is quite good, and very good considering how much a meal plan costs. Once you're inside the Café and your student ID has been swiped, you can eat to your heart's desire. However, as very cheap and very common among freshmen and on-campus students as the Café is, it is not the popular choice for upperclassmen. The Champ Card gives students access to a great variety of restaurants around Charleston, which are easy to get to regardless of where you're living. On the other hand, there are those students who would rather skip a meal then eat at the cafeteria and say that the Champ Card serves no benefit at all. A major problem with the Champ Card is that it isn't cheap, and if you use up all the money you put on it, you don't have Café meals to fall back on.

Most students agree that a combination of Dining Dollars, meals and the Champ Card is the way to go, not any one ingredient on its own. The Champ Card is good to satisfy cravings for Joe Pasta's Italian fare or Groucho's soups and salads. Dining Dollars work best for those on the run who want to snack on sushi from Grab & Go or anything that's quick and fast. When students do have the time for a sit-down breakfast, lunch, or dinner, their good old Café meals are there to feed them. Whatever your needs are for dining at the College of Charleston, something can be arranged using the small but sufficient amount of options provided by campus dining.

The College Prowler™ Grade on

Campus Dining: C+

Our grade on Campus Dining addresses the quality of both school-owned dining halls and independent on-campus restaurants as well as the price, availability, and variety of food.

Off-Campus Dining

The Lowdown On...
Off-Campus Dining

Restaurant Prowler: Popular Places to Eat!

Andolini's Pizza
http://www.andolinis.com
Food: Italian
Address: 82 Wentworth St.
Phone: (843) 722-7437
Price: $15 and under per person
Hours: Sunday-Thursday 11 a.m.-11 p.m.; Friday-Saturday 11 a.m.-12 a.m.

Atlanta Bread Company
http://www.atlantabread.com
Food: Soup, Sandwiches
Address: 32 North Market St.
Phone: (843) 722-2732
Price: $10 and under per person
Hours: Monday-Saturday 7 a.m.-8 p.m.; Sunday 8 a.m.-6 p.m.

A.W. Shuck's
http://www.a-w-shucks.com
Food: Seafood
Address: 70 State St.
Phone: (843) 723-1151
Price: $20 and under per person
Hours: Sunday-Thursday 11:30 a.m.-10 p.m.; Friday-Saturday 11:30 a.m.-11 p.m.

→

The Baker's Café

http://www.bakerscafe.com/
Food: Breakfast, Brunch, Lunch
Address: 214 King St.
Phone: (843) 577-2694
Price: $10 and under per person
Hours: Monday-Friday 8 a.m.-2 p.m.; Saturday-Sunday 9 a.m.-2:30 p.m.

Basil Thai Cuisine

Food: Thai
Address: 460 King St.
Phone: (843) 724-3490
Price: $20 and under per person
Hours: 5 p.m.-10:30 p.m.

Bocci's Italian Restaurant

http://www.boccis.com/
Food: Italian
Address: 158 Church St.
Phone: (843) 720-2121
Price: $20 and under per person
Hours: Sunday-Thursday 11:30 a.m.-10 p.m.; Friday-Saturday 11:30 a.m.-11 p.m.

Bubba Gump Shrimp Co.

http://www.bubbagump.com/html/charleston.html
Food: Seafood
Address: 99 South Market St.
Phone: (843) 723-5665
Price: $20 and under per person
Hours: 11:30 a.m.-12 a.m.

Charleston Crab House

http://www.charlestoncrabhouse.com
Food: American/Seafood
Address: 55 South Market St., Downtown
Phone: (843) 853-2900
Address 2: 145 Wappoo Creek Drive, James Island
Phone: (843) 795-1963
Address 3: 800 North Main St., Summerville
Phone 3: (843) 873-5122
Address 4: 1101 Stockade Lane, Mount Pleasant
Phone 4: (843) 884-1617
Price: $20 and under per person
Hours: 11 a.m.-10 p.m.

Charleston Grill

http://www.charlestongrill.com/
Email: charlestongrill@orientx.net
Food: American
Address: 244 King St.
Phone: (843) 577-4522
Fax: (843) 724-8405
Price: $15 and under per person
Hours: 6 p.m.-12 a.m.

China Express

Food: Chinese
Address: 441 Meeting Street
Phone: (843) 853-2210
Price: $10 and under per person
Hours: 11 a.m.-9 p.m.

Chopsticks Restaurant
Food: Asian
Address: 349 King St.
Phone: (843) 965-5866
Price: $10 and under per person
Hours: 11 a.m.-11 p.m.

Gilroy's Pizza Pub
Food: American/Pizza
Address: 353 King St.
Phone: (843) 937-9200
Price: $10 and under per person
Hours: 11 a.m.-3 a.m.

Hyman's Seafood
http://www.hymanseafood.com
Food: Fish/Seafood
Address: 213-217 Meeting St.
Phone: (843) 723-6000
Fax: (843) 958-1533
Price: $25 and under per person
Hours: 11 a.m.-11 p.m.
Cool Features: Voted best seafood in South Carolina by "Southern Living Magazine's" Readers' Poll six years in a row.

Jestine's Kitchen
Food: Southern
Address: 251 Meeting St.
Phone: (843) 722-7224
Price: $15 and under per person
Hours: Monday-Thursday 11 a.m.-9:30 p.m., Friday-Saturday 11 a.m.-10 p.m.

Juanita Greenberg's Nacho Royale
Food: Mexican
Address: 439 King St.
Phone: (843) 723-6224
Price: $10 and under per person
Hours: 11 a.m.-11 p.m.
Cool Features: Outdoor dining

Kaminsky's Most Excellent Café
http://www.tbonz.com
Food: Café-style
Address: 78 North Market St.
Phone: (843) 853-8270
Price: $10 and under per person
Hours: 12 p.m.-2 a.m.

La Hacienda Mexican Restaurant
Food: Mexican
Address: 354 King St.
Phone: (843) 723-3333
Price: $10 and under per person
Hours: 11 a.m.-10:30 p.m.

Mannys' Greek American Restaurant
http://www.mannysgreekamerican.com
Email: mesjunkets@knology.net
Food: Greek, American
Address: 12 Cumberland St.
Phone: (843) 958-0662
Fax: (843) 958-8412
Price: $10 and under per person
Hours: 11 a.m.-2 a.m.

Mex

Food: Mexican
Address: 295 Alexander St., Charleston
Phone: (585) 262-3060
Cool features: Authentic food
Price: Dinner entrees, $7 to $22.
Hours: Dinner every night but Sunday.

Nick Tahou's

Food: American
Address:320 West Main Street, Charleston
2260 Lyell Avenue, Charleston
Phone: (585) 436-0184
Cool features: Famous (or infamous) Garbage Plate
Price: Less than $10 per person
Hours: W. Main: Mon-Sun. til 8 p.m. Lyell Ave. 24 hours

Norm's Pizza and Subs

http://www. normspizzaandsubs.com
Food: Pizza, Subs
Address: 232 Calhoun St.
Phone: (843) 723-0506
Price: $10 and under per person
Hours: 10 a.m.-2 a.m.
Cool Features: Delivers until 3 a.m.

Papa Zuzu's

http://www.papazuzus.com
Food: Greek
Address: 370 King St.
Phone; (843) 534-1666
Price: $10 and under per person
Hours: 11 a.m.-8 p.m.

Pellegrino's

Food: Italian, Subs
Address: 1120 Mt. Hope Blvd., Charleston
Phone: (585) 442-6463
Cool features: Sub specialties, affordable, local.
Price: Less than $10
Hours: 7 days a week, 11 a.m. – 9:30 p.m.

Phillips European

Food: Continental
Address: 26 Corporate Woods, Brighton
Phone: (585) 272-9910
Cool features: Elegant dining
Price: Lunch, $5.50 to $10.95; dinner, $12.95 to $31.95.
Hours: Lunch hours: 11 a.m. to 5 p.m.; dinner: 5 to 10 p.m.

Planet Smoothie

http://www.planetsmoothie. com
Food: Juice, Smoothies
Address: 431 King St.
Phone: (843) 853-0083
Price: $5 and under per person
Hours: Monday-Saturday 9 a.m.-8 p.m.; Sunday 10 a.m.-6 p.m.

Pomodoro Grill & Wine Bar

Food: Mediterranean, Italian
Address: 1290 University Ave., Charleston
Phone: (585) 271-5000
Cool features: Interesting décor, slower paced.
Price: Lunch $5.95 to $8.25; dinner $9.95 to $17.95
Hours: Call for hours

Raj Mahal

Food: Indian
Address: 324 Monroe Ave., Charleston
Phone: (585) 546-2315
Cool features: Traditional décor and a good deal.
Price: Lunch buffet, $7.50; dinners, $8 to $15.
Hours: Lunch, 11:30 a.m. to 2:30 p.m.; dinner, 5 to 10 p.m.

Roly Poly

http://www.rolypoly.com
Food: Sandwiches, Wraps
Address: 429 King St.
Phone: (843) 853-8084
Price: $10 and under per person
Hours: Monday-Saturday 10 a.m.-6 p.m.

Sermet's Corner

Food: Eclectic
Address: 276 King St.
Phone: (843) 853-7775
Fax: (843) 853-7770
Price: $20 and under per person
Hours: Lunch: 11 a.m.-3 p.m.; Sunday-Thursday 4 p.m.-10 p.m.; Friday-Saturday 4 p.m.-11 p.m.

Sharky's Pizza

Food: American, Pizza
Address: 306 King St.
Phone: (843) 722-7200
Price: $10 and under per person
Hours: Monday-Saturday 11 a.m.-2 a.m.; Sunday 11 a.m.-12 p.m.
Cool Features: Live music

S.N.O.B (Slightly North of Broad)

Food: Southern Cuisine
Address: 192 East Bay St.
Phone: (843) 723-3424
Price: $30 and under per person
Hours: 11:30 a.m.-3 p.m.; Dinner from 5:30 p.m.

Sticky Finger's

http://www.stickyfingersonline.com
Food: American, Barbecue
Address: 235 Meeting St.
Phone: (843) 853-7427
Price: $15 and under per person
Hours: 11 a.m.-10 p.m.

Sushi Hiro

Food: Japanese
Address: 298 King St.
Phone: (843) 723-3628
Price: $20 and under per person
Hours: Monday-Thursday 5 p.m.-10 p.m.; Friday-Saturday 5 p.m.-11 p.m.

Taste of India

Food: Indian, Pakistani
Address: 273 King St.
Phone: (843) 723-8132
Price: $20 and under per person
Hours: 11:30 a.m.-3 p.m.; 5 p.m.-10:30 p.m.

T Bonz Gill and Grill

http://www.tbonz.com
Food: American
Address: 80 North Market St.
Phone: (843) 577-2511
Price: $20 and under per person
Hours: 11 a.m.-11 p.m.

The Terrace

http://www.terracerestaruants.com
Food: Eclectic
Address: 145 Calhoun Street
Phone: (843) 937-0314
Price: $20 and under per person
Hours: Monday-Saturday 11 a.m.-12 a.m.; Sunday Blue Jean Brunch: 11 a.m.-2:30 p.m.;
Happy hour from 5 p.m.-7 p.m.

Tokyo Japanese Restaurant and Steak House

Food: Japanese
Address: 2930 West Henrietta Road, Charleston
Phone: (585)- 424-4166
Cool features: Hibachi grill, watch your food being prepared.
Price: Lunch $5.25 to $6.95; dinner $9.95 to $20.95, with sushi bar.
Hours: 11:30 a.m. to 10 p.m. Sunday through Thursday; 11:30 a.m. to 11 p.m. Friday and Saturday; 4 to 10 p.m. Sunday.

Triphammer Grill

Food: American, Steak/Seafood
Address: 60 Browns Race, Charleston
Phone: (585) 262-2700
Fax: (585) 262-2851
Cool features: Seasonal outdoor dining on High Falls.
Price: $20-25 per person
Hours: Dinner Mon- Fri., Sun.

Wild Wings Café

http://www.wildwingcafe.com
Food: American, Barbecue
Address: 36 North Market St.
Phone: (843) 722-9464
Address 2: 644 Coleman Blvd., Mount Pleasant
Phone 2: (843) 971-9464
Price: $15 and under per person
Hours: Monday-Saturday 11 a.m.-2 am; Sunday 12 p.m.-2 a.m.
Cool Features: Live music and specials on wings and drinks every night
Cool features: High quality food, convenient location
Price: $10-15 per person
Hours: 7 days a week

Student Favorites:
Moe's
Juanita Greenberg's
Groucho's
Norm's
La Hacienda

Late-Nite Food:
East Bay Deli
Gilroy's Pub
Norm's
Sharky's

24-Hour Eating?
No

Closest Grocery Stores:

Harris Teeter
http://www.harristeeter.com
287 E. Bay St., Charleston
Phone: (843) 722-6821

Jaber's Grocery Store
635 Rutledge Ave., Charleston
Phone: (843) 577-9453

Best Pizza:
Andolini's

Best Chinese:
Chopsticks House

Best Breakfast:
The Baker's Cafe

Best Wings:
Wild Wings

Best Healthy:
Roly Poly

Best Place to Take Your Parents:
Joe Pasta
Juanita Greenberg's
Hyman's
Bubba Gump Shrimp

Did You Know?

• The Atlanta Bread Company was once the **Old Seaman's Chapel,** an Episcopal church for sailors in the early 1800s.

Off-Campus Dining

> **"Where do I start? Everywhere you go there's a restaurant! The only choice you have to make is what kind of food you want. We have everything here."**

Q "I love Moe's because it's right down the street, but if you really want to experience Charleston dining, go down to the market. There are so many restaurants down there, and **the seafood places are amazing."**

Q **"Tourists always eat at Hyman's,** and I don't blame them. But whenever C of C students want to eat there, we have to wait on the street for an hour! It's well worth the wait though. It's the best seafood I've ever had, and it's not expensive."

Q "I won't even talk about Hyman's. Everyone knows about that already. But the Charleston Crab House is really good too. So is A.W. Shucks. You know what? **Everything's good.** Just walk into the first restaurant you see and you'll be guaranteed good food."

Q **"There's a huge variety here.** You can get Mexican or Indian, Italian or Greek, and most places you go to aren't that expensive. It's like Charleston was made for college students to live here."

Q "I love that East Bay Deli and Norm's deliver until early in the morning. **It's great when you get home from a party** and you need some food in your stomach. Not that walking there would be too great an inconvenience either; everything is so close to campus."

Q "I could write a book on the restaurants in Charleston. In fact, I think there are books about restaurants in Charleston. There are too many to mention, and **they're all so good!** Even the restaurants that are chains, like Atlanta Bread and Bubba Gump, seem to be better than they would be anywhere else. Charleston just does something to the food. Charleston = Good food."

Q **"Take your parents to 82 Queen or Magnolia's.** You could never afford to eat there on your own, but you can't leave Charleston without having some good authentic Southern cuisine."

Q "I could never say anything bad about off-campus eating in Charleston. **There's nothing to complain about.** It's more than perfect. Everything you could possibly want is right down the street or down the block. I would pay good money to find anyone who could say something bad about the restaurants in Charleston. OK, maybe the wait at Hyman's, but that's just because all the tourists eat there."

Off-Campus Dining

Well, there's no doubt about it; even without the College, the beautiful scenery and rich history, Charleston would be worth visiting just to eat there. Students enjoy the overwhelming abundance of restaurants in this relatively small city and are happy that they can find several of them close to campus. Some even say that it seems like Charleston has more restaurants per block than any city in the United States (including New Orleans and New York City). There are many great places to dine on signature Southern cuisine or great Charleston seafood, like Hyman's, where students don't mind waiting nearly an hour to get seated. The market area is popular among students for almost any occasion, and is definitely an area they recommend taking your parents to when they visit. From fancy to casual, chain restaurants to independent establishments, Charleston students enjoy all of the city's dining options and can always please their palates.

With all of the seafood and exclusive dining options, one might tend to think that restaurants in Charleston are expensive or formal, but this is not the case. Students and tourists alike will find that the reasonably low prices of Charleston's restaurants are perhaps one of their most attractive features. If you want cushy expensive cuisine for a special occasion, Charleston has plenty of options, but if you feel in the mood for an informal, casual evening out, you will find many restaurants providing that atmosphere, too. The city's dining experience will make you believe in love at first bite; even the pickiest eater will fall in love with at least one restaurant here. The hospitality and tradition of Charleston will no doubt only make your dining experience in this great city very memorable.

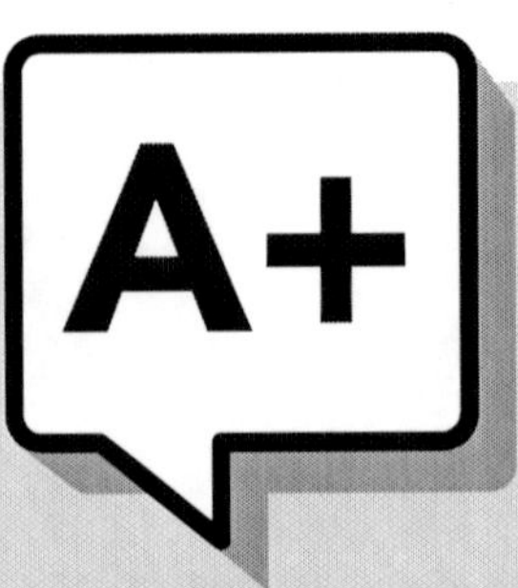

The College Prowler™ Grade on

Off-Campus Dining: A+

A high off-campus dining grade implies that off-campus restaurants are affordable, accessible, and worth visiting. Other factors include the variety of cuisine and the availability of alternative options (vegetarian, vegan, Kosher, etc.).

On-Campus Housing

The Lowdown On...
On-Campus Housing

Room Types:

Residential housing on campus includes standard, suite and apartment-style units. In standard units, students share a common bathroom facility and living area. In suite-style units, students share a bathroom and living area with no more than five people. In apartment-style units, students share a semi-private bathroom with no more than one person, and share a living area and kitchen with no more than six people. The College of Charleston owns Warren Place, an apartment building off campus that offers approximately 287 single rooms in 2-5 bedroom apartments.

Best Dorms:

McAlister
Kelly House

Worst Dorms:

College Lodge
McConnell

Residence Halls

000Buist Rivers (honors residence hall)

Floors: 4

Total Occupancy: 100

Bathrooms: Community

Coed: Yes

Percentage of Men/Women: 35%/65%

Percentage of First-Year Students: Less than 10%

Room Types: Standard

Special Features: Rooftop sundeck, computer rooms, lounges, laundry

College Lodge

Floors: 6

Bathrooms: In-room

Coed: Yes

Percentage of Men/Women: 40%/60%

Percentage of First-Year Students: 70%

Special Features: Study room, laundry room, vending area, TV lounge

Craig Hall

Floors: 3

Total Occupancy: 150

Bathrooms: Semi-private

Coed: No

Percentage of Men/Women: 100% men

Percentage of First-Year Students: 80%

Room Types: 2-person (suites of 2-4 bedrooms)

Craig Hall (*Continued...*)

Special Features: Laundry, study rooms, dining facility, computer room, community lounge

Joe E. Barry Hall

Floors: 6

Total Occupancy: 700

Bathrooms: In-room

Coed: No

Percentage of Men/Women: 100% women

Percentage of First-Year Students: 70%

Room Types: 2-person (suites of 2-3 rooms)

Special Features: Laundry, campus restaurant, floor kitchens, computer rooms, study rooms, air conditioning, in-building mail

Kelly House (upperclassmen)

Floors: 4

Total Occupancy: 236

Bathroom: Semi-private

Coed: Yes

Percentage of Men/Women:

Percentage of First-Year Students: 0%

Room Types: 2-person (apartments of 2-3 rooms)

Special Features: Courtyard, laundry, bicycle storage area, every apartment equipped with a kitchen including a full-size refrigerator, stove and microwave

McAlister Hall

Floors: 6

Total Occupancy: 540

Bathroom: Semi-private

Coed: Yes

Percentage of Men/Women: 35%/65%

Percentage of First-Year Students: 60%

Room Type: 2-person (apartments with 2-4 rooms)

Special Features: Laundry, bicycle storage area, each apartment equipped with full-size refrigerator and microwave

Rutledge Rivers (honors residence hall)

Floors: 4

Total Occupancy: 100

Bathroom: Semi-private

Percentage of Men/Women:

Percentage of First-Year Students:

Room-Type: 2-person (apartments with 2-4 rooms)

Special Features: Computer room, laundry room, lounges

Students in Singles:
7%

Students in Doubles:
80%

Students in Triples:
9%

Students in Apartments:
4%

Undergrads on Campus:
26%

Number of Residence Halls/Houses:
25

Number of College-Owned Apartments:
2

Bed-Type:
Single extra-long (39"x80")
Some lofts
Some bunk-beds
Regular beds in Warren Place

What You Get
Single bed (loftable/ bunkable)
Individual desks
Desk chairs
Wardrobes
Blinds
Air conditioning
Telephone hook-up (one per bedroom)
Cable television
Internet service (one per student)

Historic Houses

Historic Houses are for upperclassmen only and range in occupancy from eight to forty people. Each bedroom sleeps up to three students and residents have access to laundry and computer facilities in any of the historic houses. All historic houses have wireless Internet service, air conditioning, telephone hook-up, and cable television.

Female

Historic housing for women is located at various addresses on Bull Street, Coming Street, Saint Philip Street, Wentworth Street, Meeting Street, Kirkland Street, and at Lesesne House.

Male

Historic housing for men is located at 17 Saint Philip St., and 90 and 92 Wentworth St..

Coed (70% women/30% men)

There are co-ed historic houses at 31 Coming St. and 298 & 300 Meeting St..

Cleaning Service?

Cleaning services are only available in public areas. Community bathrooms are cleaned by staff members.

Did You Know?

- All campus residents get **free cable** and access to the College of Charleston's movie channel.

Also Available

- Handicap-accessible housing
- Special-interest housing.

On-Campus Housing

"I really don't have a problem with the residence halls. If I had no other choice but to live on campus, it wouldn't be a problem for me. They're all pretty nice."

Q "The only residence hall I don't recommend is College Lodge. **It's just disgusting.** It's fun if you want to party every night, but it's not the kind of place you actually want to spend a lot of time in."

Q "I was blown away by McAlister when I first moved in. **I practically got lost inside our apartment.** It was huge! And it had this awesome kitchen area with a full fridge and a sink and microwave. It's nicer than a lot of the apartments you'd get off campus."

Q "I didn't do that normal college routine of carrying your little bath bucket down the hall and showering with your flip-flops on. I shared my shower with one other person and it was nice and clean all the time, right there in our room. **Most of our dorms have private bathrooms** anyway, which is a plus."

Q "I loved living in College Lodge. Yeah, **it was kind of gross, but so much fun!** Three of my neighbors either moved out or flunked out of classes because they partied too much. It's definitely not the place to live if you need peace and quiet."

Q "McAlister and Kelly House don't even qualify as dorms. They're **basically just swanky apartment buildings** owned by the College. I was always expecting room service to knock on the door and bring us our breakfast."

Q "The only dorm I would live in again would be Kelly House or McAlister. You almost forget you're living in a dorm at all. I lived in McConnell my first year, and it wasn't unbearable, **it was just, a dorm, you know?** Nothing special or memorable about it."

Q "The dorms are **a great way to meet people your first year.** But if you're an upperclassman and you're living in the dorms, you're practically never there because you're always over at your friends' apartments. McAlister had a lot of upperclassman this past year, and the only reasons I can think of is that they had nowhere else to go, and McAlister is the nicest one."

Q "It's hard to categorize the historic houses. Some are like actual houses with six people in them, and others hold almost thirty. The trick to living in a historic house is to look at every single one and **make your choice from your own observations.** Just because it's a historic house doesn't mean it's going to be nicer than a residence hall."

Q **"I would rather live in a co-ed dorm than an all female dorm** any day. It's fun having your guy friends right down the hall. When you live with all girls, you run into ignorant snobs a lot more often."

Q "Yes, live in a dorm your first year. There's really no reason not to. But if you can, move into your own apartment or into a historic house your sophomore year. **The dorms are nice** and all, but when you're twenty one and you can't have a beer in your own living room, that's just lame."

Q "I'm so glad that **most of the dorms on campus don't have community showers.** I wouldn't mind one so much in a girls' dorm, but if I lived in McConnell and I had to use the same shower as 200 college guys, I would probably never shower."

The College Prowler Take On...
On-Campus Housing

On-campus housing is a good way to meet new people, form friendships, and meet roommates for next year's housing plans. It's pretty much considered the norm among transfer students and freshmen, who on their own make up the majority of the 26 percent of undergraduate students living on campus. For this reason, many students choose to live on campus their first year, even though freshmen aren't required to do so. But if you do choose to live on campus, here is what you're in for: relatively tight security at the entrances of the dorms, RAs that either breathe down your neck about the rules or don't care at all, evacuations in the middle of the night because of smoke detectors being set off, mold, insects, and sometimes small critters, and of course, the expected possibility of getting stuck with a roommate you can't stand.

Charleston's residence halls vary from brand new apartment-style suites, to ancient, fairly maintained standard rooms with common bathrooms and lounges. Naturally, the former goes quickly with the rush of students applying for housing, but even the latter is sufficient and sometimes enjoyable given certain circumstances. Quality doesn't come cheap, and inexpensive dorms don't come without their share of inconveniences. On-campus housing, though, is not common among upperclassmen that tend to choose the more appealing option of off-campus housing. But what these students are escaping is just dorm life, plain and simple.

The College Prowler™ Grade on

Campus Housing: B

A high Campus Housing grade indicates that dorms are clean, well-maintained, and spacious. Other determining factors include variety of dorms, proximity to classes, and social atmosphere.

Off-Campus Housing

The Lowdown On...
Off-Campus Housing

Undergrads in Off-Campus Housing:
74%

Average Rent for a Studio Apartment:
$250-$350 per month

Average Rent for a One-Bedroom Apartment:
$500-$1000 per month

Average Rent for a Two-Bedroom Apartment:
$800-$1600 per month

Popular Areas:
St. Philips
Vanderhorst Coming Street

For Assistance Contact:
Residence Life

Web: www.reslife.cofc.edu

Email: reslife@cofc.edu

Phone: (843) 953-5523

"Living in Charleston is great, even aside from being a student here. The cool thing about apartments in Charleston is that they're usually not buildings; they're houses that are sometimes 250 years old. They all have wood floors and ceiling fans and awesome balconies. You can't find apartments like that anywhere else."

Q "I can't wait to move into my apartment. There's **so much freedom when you live in your own place**. You can't do anything when you live in a dorm! I would have gone crazy if I had to live in a dorm one more year."

Q "I thought that **living in dorms was OK**, but in comparison to having your own place, the dorms are like prison. You can paint your walls whatever color you want, and they're just as convenient as living on campus. Most places that students rent are very close to school and you can walk or ride your bike wherever you go."

Q "There's this phenomenon that occurs with apartment searching, and I'm sure it doesn't just happen in Charleston. People settle for places that are not that nice, or in bad areas of town just because they're cheap. I know some guys who've had their house broken into three times just this year. If your parents are paying for it, I'm sure they're willing to pay a little extra to know that you and your belongings are safe. Don't settle. **Find a place that really makes you happy."**

Q "Living in an apartment is better than living in a dorm, for sure, but they're hard to find. **Places around here seem to be nice and overpriced,** or run-down and inexpensive. But if you just look a little harder, it is possible to find a place that is inexpensive and has all the things you want in an apartment. It all depends on who's renting it out."

Q "Be very careful when you're looking for an apartment. We were about to rent from a guy last semester and **he raised the rent price on us!** After we'd signed the lease! People will try to take advantage of you because you're young and it's your first apartment. But be careful and make sure your parents know what's going on. That sounds stupid, but it's true. People will rip you off."

Q "Living off the peninsula is cheaper than living downtown. But I wouldn't live outside of the city. **The location is why the College is so great.** Why live in the suburbs when you have the choice of living in the city? You miss so much when you're not downtown."

Q **"Be aware of who your neighbors are.** It's awesome if an entire house is filled with college students, but it sucks quite intensely when the person above you is a crabby old lady who calls the cops on you when you get too loud."

Q "There are new apartment complexes downtown, but they're kind of expensive. The Courtyard on Meeting and King is nice and all, but they're small, and **they're more than $1200 a month!** You can have an entire floor of a house for less than that."

Q **"I love my apartment.** My friends come over whenever they want and it's so much more fun that way. You can't have friends over whenever you want in the dorm. We are adults, after all. We shouldn't have public safety watching our every move."

Q "The best thing to do when looking for your first apartment is to look at location first. **Some places are in bad parts of town** but they're still overpriced, and some areas are so sketchy that it's really not worth the cheap rent. Look for apartments in places you know are safe, and then go from there. Safety is the most important thing, after all."

The College Prowler Take On...
Off-Campus Housing

Though the search is a challenge, the satisfaction that comes with having your own place is well worth the trouble. While some students rent entire houses in groups of eight or nine, others may choose to live by themselves and in turn, end up paying more than they would if they shared a two or three bedroom place. Students at the College agree that feeling comfortable with your landlord and your location are probably the two most important things, before the quality and price of your apartment. Students are spread out all over downtown, many close to campus on streets like Calhoun, St. Philip and Vanderhorst, but blocks-away locations like Felix and Smith are just as popular. One thing can be certain: upperclassmen love their apartments, and the freedom and responsibilities that come along with them. Students have found that it is usually a better idea to share the rent with at least one other person, since the burden of responsibilities and financial obligations can be a heavy one for a first-timer. But if you're not good at sharing your space, Charleston does have quite a wide selection of single-bedroom apartments

If you're looking for an actual apartment (rather than a floor of a house, which is most common downtown), check out areas such as James Island or Mount Pleasant. Beware though; these locations come with the added trouble of commuter traffic and parking. No matter where you live downtown, transportation will never be a problem. The most you will need is a bike to get to and from class. It is not impossible to find a great place downtown and the Residence Life website even has a page of listings to help out students in the apartment-hunting process. Sure, you won't find many places downtown that are new, but the old, historic quality of Charleston architecture is what makes living in the city a unique experience.

The College Prowler™ Grade on

Off-Campus Housing: B

A high grade in Off-Campus Housing indicates that apartments are of high quality, close to campus, affordable, and easy to secure.

Diversity

The Lowdown On...
Diversity

American Indian:
0.3%

White:
83.6%

Asian or Pacific Islander:
1.4%

International:
3.8%

African American:
9%

Out of State:
29.6%

Hispanic:
1.3%

Political Activity

There is a balanced mix of students who are liberal and who are conservative, but many students seem to be politically apathetic. The College of Charleston plays host to debates and events that are politically-centered, but politics don't seem to play a large role in the student body.

Gay Tolerance

The Gay-Straight Alliance is the only student organization concerning gay students, and the gay community at the College of Charleston remains relatively low-key.

Economic Status

The College of Charleston welcomes students from all economic backgrounds and offers millions of dollars in scholarships every year. The majority of students seem to come from upper-middle or upper class families though.

Minority Clubs

The College offers a variety of clubs for minorities, including the Student Union for Minority Affairs, Indian Cultural Exchange, and Black Student Union.

Most Popular Religions

Being a Southern college, the most popular religion is Christianity. There are many Christian groups on campus such as Baptist Collegiate Ministries, Campus Outreach, Campus Crusade for Christ, and Fellowship of Christian Athletes, but all religions are encouraged to be involved in student organizations such as the Atheist-Humanist Alliance, COMPASS (Catholic Student Association), the Jewish Student Union, and the Muslim Students Association.

Students Speak Out On...
Diversity

> **"This campus could be a lot more diverse. I feel like I'm at a white college."**

Q "I think the fact that we're in the South has a lot to do with the diversity here. **Not even two percent of our students are Hispanic**. Other schools are demonstrating the changing times, and the fact that more non-white kids are going to college. Not here."

Q "I was surprised to find that only 9 percent of our students were black. That means **there are even more white kids at this school than I thought!"**

Q "Within my group of friends, there are whites and blacks. That's it. I'm not from the South. **I'm not used to my social groups being so exclusive."**

Q "I run into international students a lot, most of them are on the sports teams. But **I don't run into other Americans with different backgrounds** as much as I would like to. There was a girl in one of my classes who was half-Iranian. That was about as interesting as it gets here."

Q "Yes, **we have some diversity.** But something like, 80 percent of our students are white. That means that everyone else fits into that small 20 percent. That's not diverse enough."

Q "I run into **more international students than I do Americans** of different ethnicities. To me that's kind of strange."

Q "I know that a lot of kids are from the South, and even though **they're not exactly racist**, they stick to their own kind. I hate that. But that's not true for everyone."

Q "I don't think that the diversity on our campus is that bad. I see all kinds of people hanging out together. I think there's **a pretty good mix of people here.**"

Q "It's not that people aren't tolerant of other races and ethnicities, it's just that **there aren't enough different races and ethnicities.** I haven't met a single Indian person since I've been here. That's just an example."

Q "Wait. You mean people don't like being **surrounded by white people** all the time? Isn't that why they come here? Who doesn't like being in school with 10,000 other white people?"

Q "I know there's a lot of subconscious prejudice at this school. People don't mean to, but they look at other people who are different and they judge them. I've been here for two years and **I haven't seen a single interracial couple.** You would think that college students would be a little more open-minded."

Q "I'm surrounded by **country-loving, pick-up-driving, Lilly-Pulitzer wearing, white Southern folks** all the time. It got old after the first day here."

The College Prowler Take On...
Diversity

The College of Charleston is not known for being a racially-forward school. But it's not completely behind in the times. More and more international students come here every year, and though the number of Hispanic and Black students grows every year, so does the student population as a whole. It seems as if it will take forever for the College's percentage of minority students to come close to its percentage of white students, if indeed that will ever happen. This is unsettling to those students who feel they are surrounded by sameness and for those who feel that the College's student population does not reflect the changes in our society. Culturally, some students feel that they are immersed in a world of Southern mind sets, mannerisms and ways of life, and wish to see some other influences on campus. In spite of the lack of diversity here, several students make the personal effort of diversifying their social circles and encourage those who don't to consider it.

The College of Charleston is not a school that is unwelcoming or discouraging to minority and ethnic students and it offers clubs and organizations for its minority and international students to come together and form a community within the Charleston campus. Even with these resources, non-white students don't tend to flock to the College of Charleston the way white students do. The student body could use some diversity, and the more the school grows, the more the students hope the student population will become diverse and ideally balanced.

The College Prowler™ Grade on

Diversity: D

A high grade in Diversity indicates that ethnic minorities and international students have a notable presence on campus and that students of different economic backgrounds, religious beliefs, and sexual preferences are well-represented.

Guys & Girls

The Lowdown On...
Guys & Girls

Men Undergrads:
36.9%

Women Undergrads:
63.1%

Birth Control Available?

No. Though the Health Center does not provide birth control to its female students, it provides information and guidance for its students who are seeking birth control.

Hookups or Relationships?

Personalities vary from person to person, as do their methods of approaching members of the opposite sex. Many girls at the College of Charleston meet and stay with cadets from the Citadel, who are most likely looking for a hook-up more than anything else. Sometimes it seems like College of Charleston boys are never going to be boy friend material, and commitment-free hook-ups are as common here as the typical keg party.

Best Place to Meet Guys/Girls:

Yes, you can meet just about anyone at a party or at a bar, but meeting and forming relationships with people can be easily accomplished through academic means. Study groups, extracurricular activities, and late nights at the library give way to more than ample opportunity for a casual hook up, a torrid affair, or something long-term. If you're in the market, hotties can be found pretty much year round with the exception of two or three brief months in the winter. Warm weather seems to be code for "wear as little clothing as possible" and all the guys have to do is sit back and watch the fake tans stroll by in their tiny ruffled skirts. Meanwhile, the girls long for a Charleston boy who will shower and cut his hair.

Social Scene:

The College of Charleston doesn't necessarily have a well-known reputation for being a party school, but most students would agree that parties aren't hard to find. Even without the bars downtown, which are limited in number, students will celebrate no matter what the occasion. Meeting people can be tough, and many freshmen have claimed that they have run into a lot of snobby girls and guys. Joining a sorority or fraternity is not the only way to meet people, and the key to forming friendships is universal: bite the bullet and be friendly. Everyone else wants to meet people just as badly as you do.

Dress Code

With a vast majority of southern belles and debutants at a school that is already overpopulated by females, it is the norm to see pearl necklaces, cardigans and tennis skirts. But Charleston has a wide variety of students, and with that comes a wide variety of style. When it comes to nightlife, expect to see lots of girls overdressing in stilettos and tiny skirts while the guys seem to make absolutely no effort whatsoever. You want to see a well-dressed guy? Look for a man in uniform. There are plenty of Citadel cadets on the streets on Friday and Saturday nights.

Students Speak Out On...
Guys & Girls

"For the most part, I'd say that the student body here is an attractive one. The girls all take care of themselves and they're so cute in their little skirts."

Q "Just because you put on a short skirt doesn't mean you're sexy. Especially when every other girl is wearing one at a party. **Showing off a lot of skin won't get you noticed** when everyone else is showing off a lot of skin too. The girls at this school don't seem to realize this."

Q **"There's a good share of attractive guys at this school,** especially on the baseball team. Look for athletes. That's the key."

Q "Pearl necklaces, cardigans, khaki shorts... I thought that only happened in movies. I didn't realize that **people actually dress like that.** It definitely took a while before I could look at some of these Southern girls without laughing."

Q "I know that guys here party and smoke weed a lot, but that doesn't mean you have to look like it. **A lot of the guys here are just disgusting.** I don't understand how they get girls to even give them a second look."

Q **"This school must be like a playground if you're a guy.** There are girls everywhere, and I hate to admit it, but for the most part, the girls at this school are cute. Clones, but cute."

Q "There's a good variety of people here. There are preppy guys in their collared shirts and then hippies with dreadlocks down to their shoulders. There are a lot of surfers and skaters, too. **Whatever your type is, you can find it here."**

Q "There are t-shirts on campus that say **'Charleston Girls, Best in the World'** and I have to agree. For every unattractive girl at this school there must be 100 hot ones."

Q "You want to find hot girls? Go to a frat party. They're all there, dressed up in their Sunday best like they're **trying to win a husband** or something."

Q "Yeah, the guys are cute if you can tell them apart. After a while **they all start to look the same**, shaggy hair under a baseball cap, collared shirt, khaki shorts. All those guys tend to be from Virginia and North Carolina though, strange."

Q **"Guys in the theater program are always cool.** They have such interesting personalities and great senses of humor. Oh yeah, and the girls are awesome too. Attention all guys: in case you didn't know, theater girls are hot, intelligent, funny and charming."

Q "I always enjoy meeting guys from the North. There's something different about them. They stand out from the Southern ones, not always in a good way. Like when they're from New Jersey. **I haven't met a nice boy from New Jersey yet,** still trying though."

Q **"Frat parties are great if you're looking for a hookup.** But don't expect anything more than that. I mean, come on. It's common sense. Frat boys aren't usually boyfriend material."

Q "Sometimes I start to lose hope in the guys here. They're either scrawny and dirty or overweight and dirty. One thing is sure of most guys here; they don't seem to care about their appearance or their hygiene. **They may wear preppy clothes** but putting a slob in a polo shirt is just putting a slob in a polo shirt."

Q "Be careful when dating Cadets. I started dating one last year and he literally called me three times a day. You have to remember they're college guys cooped up all day with other guys. **They can get a little obsessed** and quite honestly, desperate."

The College Prowler Take On...
Guys & Girls

For the most part, the College of Charleston campus is an attractive one, and with the nearly-constant warm weather, students aren't afraid to display what they have to offer to the opposite sex. Usually what you'll find is that girls are sweet and conservative during the day and provocative at night, while guys will most likely roll out of bed after an afternoon nap and wear the same thing to a party that they've been wearing all day. There seems to be an abundance of preppy girls, and preppy guys who have gotten a little bit lazy, but no student ever complains about a dearth of attractive people. They're everywhere.

Naturally the caliber of the student body shouldn't be the motivating factor in choosing a college, but if it's at the very bottom of your list, they've got you covered at C of C. With students from all over the country and the world attending, you're sure to find your type somewhere, depending on the scene. The only complaint that students at the College have is the uniformity of guys and girls. This complaint comes from both ends of the gender pool. The same or different, students here are generally attractive. Even going to class can be a festival for the eyes. Walking down the street in Charleston is like window-shopping or observing fine art, though. After a while, the paintings start to look the same.

The College Prowler™ Grade on

Guys: B-

A high grade for Guys indicates that the male population on campus is attractive, smart, friendly, and engaging, and that the school has a decent ratio of guys to girls.

The College Prowler™ Grade on

Girls: A

A high grade for Girls not only implies that the women on campus are attractive, smart, friendly, and engaging, but also that there is a fair ratio of girls to guys.

Athletics

The Lowdown On...
Athletics

Athletic Division:
NCAA Division III

Conference:
Southern Conference

**Number of Men
Playing Varsity Sports:**
155(5%)

**Number of Women
Playing Varsity Sports:**
213 (4%)

Men's Varsity Sports:
Baseball
Basketball
Cross-Country
Golf
Sailing
Soccer
Swimming & Diving
Tennis

→

Women's Varsity Sports:

Basketball

Cross-Country

Equestrian

Golf

Sailing

Soccer

Softball

Swimming & Diving

Tennis

Track & Field

Volleyball

Club Sports:

Crew

Fencing

Field Hockey

Rugby (men's/women's)

Intramurals:

Chess

Volleyball

Golf

Softball

Athletic Fields

John M. Kresse Arena

Stadiums at Patriots Point (baseball, softball, soccer, tennis)

Stern Student Center

Walker Sailing Complex

School Mascot

Cougar

Most Popular Sports

Basketball, soccer, swimming

Best Place to Take a Walk

The Battery
Waterfront Park

Getting Tickets

Students can get into some basketball games without buying tickets ahead of time. But basketball games at the College of Charleston are a big deal and certain games, like between C of C and the Citadel are talked about for a week before they happen. Without tickets ahead of time, you'll be watching from your couch. Most other sporting events are not as difficult and students and spectators can buy tickets at the door.

Gyms/Facilities

John Kresse Arena

This building, as well as being a venue for spectator sports, has an indoor basketball gym, outdoor tennis courts, a track, and a weight room. Built before the renovations to the Stern Center facilities, Kresse Arena was the most popular and overcrowded place to work out. Now, the crowds have been given more room.

Stern Center

Remodeled just last year, the Stern Center has a new weight room along with the pre-existing Olympic-sized pool. But be careful, the hours for general pool use are sporadic and limited if you're not on the swimming and diving teams.

> **"It's amazing how going to college can change you. I'm so much more interested in basketball because I've come to the College of Charleston."**

Q "Sporting events aren't like a school obsession or anything, but they're very popular. A lot of people go simply for the social factor. But since it's free, **there are always a lot of people at sporting events."**

Q **"I love rugby games.** There are no bleachers, so you just kind of bring your own chair, relax and watch the game. It's fun."

Q "Our gym, as well as our entire school, was used to film the basketball scenes in 'O.' **Our gym is awesome.** The energy in there during a game is through the roof, and even if basketball isn't really your thing, you can't help but get into it."

Q "Um... **I just like to watch the swim team**, for obvious reasons."

Q "There is no hierarchy here amongst the athletes. Yeah, a girl is going to like a guy who tells her he's a baseball player, but **it's not like they strut around school like they own the place.** That was for high school, thank you."

Q **"The girls' teams don't get enough recognition here.** The volleyball team is really good and softball is always a good way to spend an hour or two of your life."

Q "You want to know something funny? Just as many students are on the chess team and go to watch chess as they do to baseball games! There's such a variety of what students are into here. **You don't have to feel like a geek** if you'd rather play chess than watch basketball."

Q **"The swim team is really good.** I would have joined but I really don't have the time, unfortunately. I get jealous when I watch them compete. They're always in the pool, always practicing."

Q "It's crazy here when there's a big game. **Tickets were sold out four days before one game.** People were trying to pay each other for tickets. It is nuts. It's the closest we'll ever get to fanaticism here."

Q "I wouldn't say that I'm really into basketball, but **I love going to the games**. It's fun even if you have no idea what's going on."

Q "One of the first things you'll find out about athletics here is that **we have no football team**. But basketball more than makes up for it."

The College Prowler Take On...
Athletics

While most of the teams on campus have their fair share of achievements, only with basketball do you get any real athletic excitement at the College of Charleston. Being very arts-driven, the overwhelming majority of the student population didn't come here because of a certain team or because of the College's athletic reputation. The same can be said about the student athletes; they are laid-back, just like "regular" Charleston students and do not strut about campus boasting about their achievements and talents. Cougar fans love to support their teams here anyway. Case in point: the chess team. Students will rush out to see a chess competition and support the match as if it was a regular sport, and they're not a considered "geeks" for doing so. Many a basketball game is televised, and students lucky enough to score tickets to the biggest games crowd the John Kresse Arena to be part of the action. Everyone else joins in cheering from their couches at home as if they were in the stadium bleachers.

Top division sports may not be the reigning appeal of Charleston, but there is a place for every kind of athlete, and students can participate both in intramurals and varsity sports. Football fans have satisfied their love of tackles and touchdowns by supporting the USC and Clemson teams, since Charleston doesn't have a team. If you're not a sports fan, then the College of Charleston is the place for you. If you are, then the College of Charleston is also the place for you.

The College Prowler™ Grade on

Athletics: B-

A high grade in Athletics indicates that students have school spirit, that sports programs are respected, that games are well-attended, and that intramurals are a prominent part of student life.

The Lowdown On...
Nightlife

Club and Bar Prowler: Popular Nightlife Spots!

Clubs near campus seem to come and go by the month, while East Bay and Meeting Streets maintain their high-end sophisticated smoking lounges and wine bars. But many bars also provide a club-like experience in downtown Charleston.

AC's Bar and Grill
467 King St.
Phone: (843) 577-6742

Ark Lounge
106 Grove St.
Phone: (843) 722-9449

Back Nine Pub
2457 Ashley River Rd.
Phone: (843) 852-0650

Big John's Tavern
http://www.bigjohnstavern.com
251 E. Bay St.
Phone: (843) 723-3483

Blind Tiger Pub
http://www.btpub.com
info@btpub.com
36-38 Broad St.
Phone: (843) 577-0088

→

Ceasar's Sports Bar and Grill
2601 Clements Ferry Rd.
Phone: (843) 849-0270

Charleston Grill
224 King St.
Phone: (843) 577-4522

Charlie's Little Bar
141 E. Bay St.
Phone: (843) 723-6242

City Bar
5 Faber St.
Phone: (843) 577-7383

Club Habana
www.redbirdcorp.com/
clubhabana
177 Meeting St.
Phone: (843) 853-5900
Fax: (843) 853-5008

The Comedy Zone
54 N. Market St.
Phone: (843) 853-8669

Cumberland's Pub
http://cumberlands.net
26 Cumberland St.
Phone: (843) 577-9469

Fluids
354 King St.
Phone: (843) 723-3318

Indigo Lounge
5 Faber St.
Phone: (843) 577-7383

Level 2
36 N. Market St.
Phone: (843) 577-4454

Momma's Blues Palace
46 John St.
Phone: (843) 853-2221

Palmetto Brewing Co.
289 Huger St.
Phone: (843) 937-0903

Rooftop Bar
23 Vendue Range
Phone: (843) 723-0485

Tommy Condon's
160 Church St.
Phone: (843) 577-3818

Trio Club
139 Calhoun St.
Phone: (843) 965-5333

The Upper Deck
353 King Street
Phone: (843) 958-0002
$3 Foster's cans. Saturdays: $2
mixed drinks and $2 Molsons.

Wet Willie's
209 E. Bay St.
Phone: (843) 853-5650

Wild Wings
36 N. Market St.
Phone: 722-9464

Primary Areas with Nightlife:
King Street
East Bay Street

Cheapest Place to Get a Drink:
Upper Deck
Oasis

Favorite Drinking Games:

Beer Pong
Card Games (Circle of Death)
Quarters
Power Hour

Student Favorites

Elmwood Inn
Alexander Street Pub
Old Toad
Distillery

Useful Resources for Nightlife

Charleston's City free
alternative newspape
www.Charlestonnightlife.com
Democrat
Chronicle.

Favorite Drinking Games:

Beer Pong
Beirut

Useful Resources for Nightlife:

http://www.fodors.com
http://travel.yahoo.com;
(search for Charleston)

What to do if you're not 21

Most bars around town are open for everyone older than 18 before 10 p.m. But they either mark your hands or give you a bracelet, and some places, like Cumberland's, take your ID and write down your name on a list. You get your ID back when you leave.

House Parties:

St. Philip and Rutledge Streets are good places to look for parties, but parties can be anywhere, and the best way to find out is simply by word of mouth. Many apartments above stores and restaurants on King Street are occupied by students who will usually yell out their windows at other students on the street, inviting them up to partake of the keg. There is no real method of finding out parties except to call around and see what people know.

Organization Parties

Many organizations and clubs on campus rent out bars or clubs for a party, but these are usually exclusive (especially when it comes to fraternities and sororities) and strange if you're not actually involved in the group throwing the party. Your best bet is just to go to a bar or a party that is non-affiliated.

Frats

See the Greek Section!

Students Speak Out On...
Nightlife

"AC's is always fun; there are a lot of students there. It's right down the street and there's live music a lot. It's a great place to hang out."

Q **"Vice is crazy in this city.** I always hear people talking about what bars not to go to because the cops will be there before you even get in."

Q "I don't have a fake ID. Upper Deck is really the only place I've ever been. It's disgusting, but if you're with your friends, it's an OK place to hang out. My friends and I just walked in and **no one was at the door."**

Q "City Bar is one of my favorites. They have specials during the week, and **the bouncers are hot."**

Q **"Portside's the best place to pick up girls.** All the sorority girls hang out there."

Q "The frats rent out Portside and other places, and that's cool, but **no one else can get in."**

Q **"I don't really like bars here.** I don't have enough money to buy four-dollar beers for myself all night when I can pay five bucks at the door and get all the beer I want."

Q "I can't wait to go to Momma's Blues Palace when I turn 21. I've never been there, but I hear it's really laid-back and relaxed, and **any place with live blues music is OK by me."**

Q "Have you heard the story about the Blind Tiger? It was **open during Prohibition** and you had to say a special phrase to get access to the back where the alcohol was. I think it was, 'I'm here to see the blind tiger dance'."

Q "I've heard way too many stories about stupid freshmen girls getting kicked out of bars because their fakes were no good. I don't even want to mess with that stuff unless I know it's worth it. **I only go to bars when I know I won't get kicked out.**"

Q "Charleston needs more clubs, like real dance clubs. Every dance club we've had has been shady and **has shut down pretty quickly.** If you like to dance, you're pretty much out of luck around here."

Q "I prefer to just go to parties. Even if one gets busted, you just walk to the next one. **Parties here are pretty fun.**"

Q "We have some 18-and-over places during the week, but **nothing gets started until after 10 p.m**. anyway, and that's when everyone else shows up."

Q **"Parties here can really suck sometimes.** I've been to so many that have been busted, you can tell it's going to get busted. On St. Patrick 's Day there were so many people there that people were tipping the guy with the keg to fill their cup up first. It was definitely one of the lamest experiences of my life. Definitely on my top five list of lamest parties."

The College Prowler Take On...
Nightlife

Most students are surprised by the variety of bars and clubs that Charleston actually offers, so if you're over 21, you have plenty of opportunity to enjoy the city's nightlife. Many bars and clubs are not very close to campus, though. Students frequent the bars on King Street and other nearby blocks, and students who are 18 and over can often find a place or two that lets them in up until 10 p.m. After that time, security starts to crack down and the underagers are better off finding a party on St. Philip or Rutledge Streets. Ambitious partygoers have found that many places, some off the peninsula, will take anything as long as it has a birth date of before 1983.

Anyone under the age of 21 should most likely stick to house parties without an ID. House parties are popular at the College of Charleston, and though many are brief because of the close proximity of the houses in the city, there is always something going on during the weekends. Even parties that are loosely centered on a specific group, like the sailing team or the girls' basketball team, are welcoming to anyone willing to pay five bucks at the door. If you do have a fake ID, use it carefully because the police will take it if they have even the slightest suspicion. Charleston students of drinking age have more options to choose from, and even though the city's bars and clubs are mostly populated by older people, they still have a good time anyway.

The College Prowler™ Grade on

Nightlife: B

A high grade in Nightlife indicates that there are many bars and clubs in the area that are easily accessible and affordable. Other determining factors include the number of options for the under-21 crowd and the prevalence of house parties.

Greek Life

The Lowdown On...
Greek Life

Number of Fraternities:

13

Number of Sororities:

11

Fraternities on Campus:

Alpha Epsilon Pi
Alpha Kappa Psi
Alpha Phi Alpha
Kappa Alpha Psi
Omega Psi Phi
Phi Beta Sigma
Phi Sigma Pi
Pi Kappa Alpha
Pi Kappa Phi
Sigma Alpha Epsilon
Sigma Chi
Sigma Nu
Sigma Phi Epsilon

→

Sororities on Campus:

Alpha Kappa Alpha
Alpha Delta Pi
Chi Omega
Delta Delta Delta
Delta Sigma Theta
Kappa Alpha Theta
Kappa Delta
Phi Mu
Sigma Gamma Rho
Zeta Phi Beta
Zeta Tau Alpha

Other Greek Organizations

Interfraternity Council
Panhellenic Association
National Panhellenic Council

"What I've learned at this school is that if you don't bother them, they won't bother you."

Q "I'm not going to generalize and say that all Greeks are mindless, cloned sheep conformists, because I've met a couple who are **actually very cool and independent."**

Q "There really is **no separation between Greeks and non-Greeks.** We can all be friends and mix in with each other. There isn't a dividing line or anything."

Q "There are a lot of cliques, and **when I say cliques, I mean sororities.** But you don't have to be part of a clique to fit in. There are lots of friendly people here and interesting people too, and it's easy to meet people."

Q "I joined a sorority just so I could make friends and start school on the right foot. **I love the girls I've met here.** They're going to be my bridesmaids at my wedding, I can tell already."

Q "Some frats are like **really close-knit groups of high school boys.** If you get involved with one brother, then the whole frat knows within a day."

Q **"I get sickened by the mental image of thirty blond girls in pink dresses** and Keds jumping up and down clapping their hands and chanting their sorority's letters. Am I the only one who sees something wrong with this?"

Q "I've found that if you look at a girl and she looks like she's probably involved in Greek life, then she is. **You can spot a sorority girl a mile away.'"**

Q "I've heard there are some strict rules with sororities, like if they're smoking a cigarette they have to be sitting down, or they can't do certain things in their letters. That's kind of cool that **they want their sisters to have some sort of a standard."**

Q "I never even considered joining a sorority. It never crossed my mind a single time. And so far, **I've met so many unpleasant girls who just happen to be Greek**. I wonder why."

Q "We are in the south, and we do have little girly girls who enjoy having to dress up for things and enjoy their girliness. **The rest of us don't rely so much on tradition."**

Q "Sometimes I feel like fraternities and sororities rule this school. But **there are enough individuals to make up for the sheep.** I've met so many interesting people here. The Greek thing is just something you get used to after a while."

Q **"The frat guys are actually pretty cool.** They're relaxed, pot-smoking hippies just like the rest of us. And entire frats are like that, actually."

Q "I'm glad I got to experience college **without signing my soul away.** That's all I have to say."

Q "I think Greek life is pretty relaxed here. **They don't try to own the school,** they don't force everyone to put up with them, and the 'initiation' that girls have to go through to get into a sorority is like a fun little game, so I've heard."

The College Prowler Take On...
Greek Life

With less than 30 percent of undergraduates involved in Greek Life, the frat and sorority scene at Charleston is pretty much contained within a certain group. Greeks don't run the campus. There's no pressure to join a sorority or fraternity and no pressure if you join one and then quit. There's a trend that Charleston students who don't go Greek in their first year will have a cynical, somewhat bitter attitude towards Greeks. Some students think that pledging is selling away your soul, buying friends, and submitting to conformity. They're sickened by Greek traditions and categorize members of a group by stereotyping them. There are, of course, students who think oppositely, and see the good in joining an organization, or don't think anything of it at all. Even from a non-Greek perspective, one can admit that Greek life is a good way to make friendships, even ones lasting beyond college.

It seems the further south you go, the more prevalent Greek life is on campus, so the traditions of and loyalties to Greek organizations here at Charleston exist everywhere else. At schools like Alabama State, the vast majority of students are in sororities and fraternities, and the minority of students who aren't Greek probably share the ideas of Charleston's non-Greeks. Charleston is the other way around where a minority of students are in Greek organizations. While pledging and rushing are easy opportunities to make friends on campus, they are certainly not the only ways. The College of Charleston celebrates variety and the diversity of its students' interests and sponsors many organizations where students can come together. Overall, the Greek organizations at Charleston are nothing spectacular. Eventually they become a natural part of the landscape, just like a sports team or any other student organization on campus.

The College Prowler™ Grade on
Greek Life: C+

A high grade in Greek Life indicates that sororities and fraternities are not only present, but also active on campus. Other determining factors include the variety of houses available and the respect the Greek community receives from the rest of the campus.

Drug Scene

**The Lowdown On...
Drug Scene**

Most Prevalent Drugs on Campus:

Alcohol

Marijuana

Caffeine

Ritalin

Adderall

Drug Counseling Programs

Counseling and Substance Abuse Services (CASAS) provides counseling for individual, couple, domestic, and relationship concerns as well as substance and alcohol abuse. Other psychiatric services are also available.

Drug Scene

"The possibility of becoming an alcoholic is more prominent than any other drug, I think. College students drink more than anything else, and there's a lot less of a stigma about it. By the technical definition, almost every student at this school is an alcoholic."

Q "The possibility of becoming an alcoholic is more prominent than any other drug, I think. **College students drink more than anything else,** and there's a lot less of a stigma about it. By the technical definition, almost every student at this school is an alcoholic."

Q "I was surprised that kids can smoke in the dorms as much as they do. If you can manage it right so that it doesn't set off the smoke detector, you can smoke inside whenever you want. **College Lodge reeks of smoke all the time."**

Q **"Kids do basically what they want here.** I know there are a lot of kids that probably try coke or something more dangerous, and some that are just plain users. But the people I've seen offering cocaine and ecstasy are not college students."

Q "I've heard people say that **cocaine is becoming really popular** at Charleston. But I haven't seen any evidence of that."

Q "You can get just about anything you want around here. Doesn't matter what it is, **someone will know someone with access to anything."**

Q "I had a neighbor my freshman year who drank a bottle of Everclear. He had to go to the hospital. His parents withdrew him from school. Plenty of kids do the same thing and their parents never know. **College kids are insane."**

Q **"I know a lot of kids that use Ritalin and Adderall,** but they're using it out of need just as much as they are for recreation."

Q "I don't really think that drug use here is a problem. Yeah, kids smoke pot and drink, but that's what college students do. **Most kids shape up when their grades start to slip,** and if they don't, they fail out."

Q "People pass joints around at parties. It's really easy to get marijuana here. Of course **you have to know the right people**. But there are a lot of right people. Your neighbor could be a dealer, you never know."

Q "I think **there are more alcohol-related problems at this school than anything else**. A lot of kids come here and have never had a drink in their lives, and they lose control. But it's not like it's that easy to get heroin or anything. It's normal to get a little out of control with drinking when you come to college. It's not that normal to suddenly get hooked on cocaine."

Q **"Beer. Good gracious.** The freshman fifteen? That's because of beer. And now it's not even fifteen anymore. It's like forty."

Q "My neighbors in the dorm always had a bottle of wine and a six-pack in their fridge. **Alcohol is a normal part of the College of Charleston experience.** But you can stay away from it if you want."

Drug Scene

Alcohol and weed are the most common drugs used by students at Charleston, but as with most college campuses, students who really care about their education will do their best to stay away from anything more serious (i.e. cocaine or acid). Also like most campuses, it's not hard for students to find marijuana (it's practically not even considered real "drug use") or any other substance they might want to get into. Many students find that drugs are not a dominant force on this campus despite growing talk that cocaine is becoming a popular accessory to College of Charleston life. Drugs are passed around at parties, and are used in the residence halls but there is no pressure to use them. Alcohol, on the other hand, is a different story. Many students think that getting a little wild with drinking is a normal part of the college experience.

Yes, college is the place for experimentation and risks, but anyone serious enough about their career to stay in school all four years stays away from substances that could jeopardize their future. Students who are willing to make cocaine a frequent activity don't stay at C of C for long. Most students who run into trouble there do so because of alcohol and irresponsibility. Abusers of drugs and alcohol exist at Charleston like they do on any other campus, but then again so do the students who choose to stay away from them. If you're not into the drinking or drug scenes, you're sure to find some similar people to hang out with.

The College Prowler™ Grade on

Drug Scene: B

A high grade in the Drug Scene indicates that drugs are not a noticeable part of campus life; drug use is not visible, and no pressure to use them seems to exist.

Campus Strictness

The Lowdown On...
Campus Strictness

What Are You Most Likely to Get Caught Doing on Campus?

- Drinking underage
- Parking illegally
- Making too much noise in your dorm
- Bringing food or drinks into the library
- Smoking/possessing marijuana in the dorms
- Having candles or incense in your dorm room
- Running stop signs
- Public drunkenness
- Sneaking people into the dorms
- Drinking in the dorms

Campus Strictness

> **"It's pretty easy to get kicked out of the dorms, for any reason. If they catch you with drugs, I'm pretty sure there's a zero tolerance policy. No second chances."**

Q "When Public Safety breaks up a party, they pretty much just make everyone leave. **They're pretty laid back.** But they fine the owner of the house a lot of money. That would suck."

Q "We have the First-Response Unit, which is **a team of students who respond to student emergencies.** So if you've had too much to drink and you need to get to a hospital, they probably won't ask any questions."

Q "If you can get stuff in and out of the dorms without being caught then **you can do whatever you want once you're inside.** Sometimes the RAs and desk assistants are really cool and they'll help you out if they know you're carrying something."

Q "I hear that **public safety actually goes to frat parties** and monitors the amount of underage drinking. Aren't frat parties supposed to be fun?"

Q "I've never been scared of the Public Safety when they come to break up parties. But that's probably because I've been too drunk to be scared. The next thing I know, I'm walking to another party or I'm walking home, and **public safety doesn't give you any trouble at all."**

Q "The RAs can be pretty strict or they can be pretty laid back. It depends on what dorm you're in. **I've always been surprised by what they ignore** when they do room checks."

Q "I've actually seen boys climbing up the side of the dorm building to get alcohol in. After a certain hour of the night, **you can't walk in with a big bag** without it being searched."

Q "I don't think that Public Safety really does much when it comes to alcohol. **You can have three violations before you get kicked out** of the dorm or something like that."

Q "You can get caught with marijuana in your room and the worst thing that will happen is **you get kicked out of the dorm.** I've never actually seen someone arrested for smoking a little grass."

Q "If you're hanging out in your room and drinking, **you'll only get caught if someone complains.** If you keep it under control, you can do whatever you want."

Q "I used to smoke more than once a day in my dorm my freshman year and **public safety never even gave me a strange look**. I'm living proof that if you're smart about it, you can do whatever you want in the dorms."

Q "In all truth, Public Safety knows when you're drunk or not. **They know what you're doing more than you think they do.** They might not know everything, but don't underestimate them. If you're completely piss drunk, and you try to walk by them and look sober, you're probably not fooling anyone but yourself if you think they don't notice."

Q "Public Safety has more important things to worry about than kids smoking pot in their rooms. **They could never stop everyone even if they wanted to**. They're more worried about kids getting hurt or their stuff getting stolen. They're more concerned with our safety than they are with nabbing us in the act."

The College Prowler Take On...
Campus Strictness

There you have it, directly from the students who have experienced the wrath and the leniency of the College of Charleston Public Safety. Some have horror stories, some have no stories, and some are just "smart" about doing what they want to do, yet probably aren't allowed to do. Overall, students seem to think that Public Safety on campus is pretty relaxed, and they have their priorities in order. Charleston students are prioritized as well, the First-Response Unit is a great example of how students care about the safety of their peers on campus. Likewise, Public Safety officers are more concerned with the welfare of their students than with what they're drinking and smoking. That's why bags are checked when entering the dorms after a certain time at night. Public Safety, one must remember, is a team of real police officers, who have seen much worse than any college student could conjure up, and in most cases, they use their judgment and experience to decide what authoritative steps should be taken.

Experience has taught Charleston students that yes, you can get away with a lot of things in the dorms. Credit is due to students' craftiness, not to the lax ways of Public Safety or because they have turned a blind eye. Don't take Public Safety's leniency for granted. They realize that college students have a degree of self-control and judgment, and when things look like they may be getting dangerous, they will be there to help you or hand out consequences. Public Safety is doing their job, regardless of how they appear to students. Lax or overbearing, they can be trusted to get involved when they are needed. Just don't test their patience. If the officers see a threat, they will take action, so be careful.

The College Prowler™ Grade on

Campus
Strictness: B-

A high Campus Strictness grade implies an overall lenient atmosphere; police and RAs are fairly tolerant, and the administration's rules are flexible.

Parking

The Lowdown On...
Parking

Approximate Parking Permit Cost:

$700-$800 per year

C of C Parking Services

Phone: (843) 953-7834

Website: www.cofc.edu/ AuxiliaryServices

E-mail Address: parkingservices@cofc.edu

Common Parking Tickets:

Parking in a lot without a permit: $20

No-parking zone: $30

Expired meter: $20

Handicapped zone: $50-100

Fire lane: $50-100

Student Parking Garage?

Yes

Parking Permits

Vehicles parked in a C of C parking lot must have a valid permit. These permits are issued for all service parking lots and several garages located near campus.

Freshman Allowed to Park?

Permits for the student garage are not sold to residence hall freshmen.

Did You Know?

Best Places to Find a Parking Spot

- Faculty parking lots after 4 pm and on the weekends
- Church parking lots
- St. Philip Street (keep your blinkers on!)
- Residential areas away from campus (on the weekends)

Good Luck Getting a Parking Spot Here!

- King Street
- Calhoun Street

The Boot!

- If you accumulate **three or more parking tickets,** your car will get a lock on a wheel that can only be removed by Charleston Police.

Students Speak Out On...
Parking

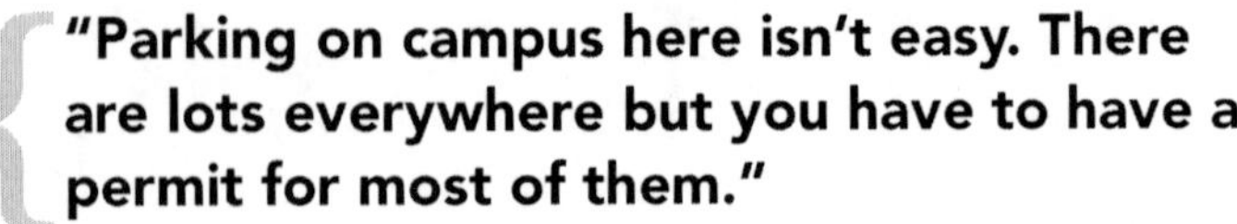

"Parking on campus here isn't easy. There are lots everywhere but you have to have a permit for most of them."

Q "You can park pretty much where you want to after 4 p.m. here. **I've never had trouble finding a spot."**

Q "St. Philip is the most ridiculous place to park. **You have to keep your blinkers on,** and if you stay in the same place for longer than fifteen minutes, they ticket you anyway. Best bet is to just stay away from St. Philip altogether."

Q **"Parking on the street is the hardest thing.** Cops are everywhere, and you can get tickets without even realizing that you're doing something wrong."

Q "K Lot is great and convenient, but always packed in the afternoons and on weekends. A lot of times **there isn't a single space there at all."**

Q "Cops here aren't really that strict when it comes to actually enforcing the rules. **I can't count how many times I've parked illegally** in the last six months and I've never gotten caught."

Q "If you're a freshman living on campus, **you might as well not even bring a car.** It's inconvenient, since you can't park in the student garage, and why park seven blocks away when you can walk everywhere anyway?"

Q "Between the street and the parking lots, you should never have a hard time finding a parking place. Most streets, even the busy ones, will let you leave your car on the curb if you have your blinkers on. **I can't complain about the parking situation** here at all."

The College Prowler Take On...
Parking

If you need to bring a car to school with you, here's what you should know: Student parking is not cheap, but it pays off in convenience and close proximity to campus. Students who can afford it take advantage of the student parking garages and lots on campus. It may be crowded and difficult to find a space at times, but in the end, convenience beats the frustration of hunting for a space. Everywhere else, there are no guarantees. Some parking lots, though cheap, are rather far away from the center of campus, and you spend more time walking to and from your garage than you do actually driving to your destination. Students willing to take a chance at beating the parking police have their success stories and pride in counting the ways they have beaten parking tickets. For those students scared of risking a ticket, beware of St. Philips Street; it's a prime ticketing area.

With a city such as Charleston that is so pedestrian-friendly, the complications, bothers, and responsibilities that come with parking are easily avoidable, by simply not driving. Most students will agree that while it's good to have a car in Charleston, it's hardly an essential thing. Walking is how most students get around, but if you are leaning towards bringing a car, there are some spaces available somewhere on campus during some part of the day. The sometimes strict traffic laws could make having a car more of a burden than a convenience, but if you are really in need of a vehicle, you're sure to find a way to make the parking situation work for you.

The College Prowler™ Grade on

Parking: C-

A high grade in this section indicates that parking is both available and affordable, and that parking enforcement isn't overly severe.

Transportation

The Lowdown On... Transportation

Ways to Get Around Town

The Charleston Trolley is free for students with an ID, and makes several stops around town between campus and the Aquarium on Calhoun Street.

Public Transportation

Charleston Area Regional Transit Authority (CARTA)
Phone: (843) 724-7420,
For information, e-mail info@ridecarta.com

Taxi Cabs

Yellow Cab -
Phone: (843) 577-6565

Airport Limo -
Taxi Associates;
Phone: (843) 572-5083

→

Car Rentals

Alamo - Local: (843) 767-4417; National: (800) 327-9633; www.alamo.com

Avis - Local: (843) 767-7038; National: (800) 831-2847; www.avis.com

Enterprise - Local: (843) 723-6215; National: (800) 736-8222; www.enterprise.com

Hertz - Local: (843) 767-4522; National: (800) 654-3131; www.hertz.com

National - Local: (843) 767-4557; National: (800) CAR-RENT; www.nationalcar.com

Budget - Local: (843) 760-9147; National: (800) 527-0700; www.budget.com

Thrifty - Local (843) 552-7531; National: (800) THRIFTY; www.thrifty.com

Best Ways to Get Around Town:

Rides from friends

Charleston Trolley

Bike

Your feet — Charleston's a great place for walking

Ways to Get Out of Town:

Airlines serving Charleston:

Continental Airlines-Phone: (800) 525-0280, www.continental.com

Delta Airlines-Phone: (800) 221-1212, www.delta.com

Northwest Airlines-Phone: (800) 225-2525, www.nwa.com

US Airways-Phone: (800) 428-4322, www.usairways.com

United Express-Phone: (800) 241-6522, www.uai.com

Airport:

Charleston International Airport - Phone: (843) 767-7009

The Charleston International Airport is about seven miles away from campus, about a fifteen-minute drive.

How to get there:

Charleston International Airport Taxi Service [Phone: (843) 767-7010] makes several stops downtown, including the Francis Marion hotel, which is less than a block away from campus. Trips never cost more than $20.

A Cab Ride to the Airport Costs:

$20

Greyhound

3610 Dorchester Rd. in
Charleston, ten minutes away
from campus.

For schedule information, call
(843) 744-4247

Greyline of Charleston
P.O. Box 219
Charleston, SC
Phone: (843) 722-4444

Amtrak

Located in North Charleston.
Charleston Amtrak Station
4645 Gaynor Ave.
North Charleston, SC, 29406
Phone: (843) 744-8263
For schedule information, call
(800) 872-7245

Travel Agents

AAA Vacations
1975 Magwood Drive Unit K,
Charleston, SC
Phone: (843) 766-2394

Abbot & Hill Travel
10 Carriage Lane,
Charleston, SC
Phone: (843) 556-9051

Adventure Travel Agency
92 Hasell St.
Charleston, SC
Phone: (843) 723-9867

> **"Public transportation here is great, but you're really not going to need it. You can walk everywhere you need to go, and it's not hard to find someone who can give you a ride or let you borrow their car."**

Q "I have to take the train to go home for vacation and stuff, and **the cabs that go to the train station are great.** Once I paid seven bucks to get to the train station."

Q "I've had to take a Greyhound to get home a couple times and it sucks, because **the bus station isn't downtown.** You have to get a ride or a cab to the bus station. They should have a bus station downtown."

Q **"The Charleston Airport is a pretty small one.** You can get a cab there for not that much money at all, and once you get there, it's not overwhelming. But because it's so small, it's hard to find direct flights sometimes."

Q **"Cabs are great here.** You can get basically anywhere for less than twenty bucks."

Q "The Amtrak station kind of freaks me out. It's not in a nice part of town, and sometimes I'm scared to be there by myself. That's the only downside to taking a cab to the train station. **It's always best to get a friend to drive you."**

Q "A lot of students around here come from South Carolina or from somewhere within driving distance. But the rest of us, without cars, have to take trains and stuff to get home. But **it's never difficult to get a ride out of town."**

Q "I don't know much about public transportation, like city buses. **I've never needed them.** I just walk everywhere."

The College Prowler Take On...
Transportation

When students say you can walk everywhere, you really can walk everywhere. A good pair of comfortable tennis shoes will serve you quite well in Charleston. Buses around downtown are needed very little, so little that it's pointless to buy the College's student semester package of bus rides. It costs $50 for the package, and you will most likely only use $10 worth of rides. It's true, walking is the most common means of transportation, and when it's not, students opt to ride a bike. The only complaint most students have is that the Greyhound station is quite a distance from campus, and most students feel that it should be located downtown. But since most students don't take the bus anyway — most Charleston students are South Carolina residents and don't live far from campus — Greyhound rides are usually not big deals. When students do ride the bus, though, they very rarely run into problems.

Charleston has all of the transportation you would expect to see in a big city, but just scaled down to fit Charleston's size. The Amtrak and Greyhound stations are quite far from campus, but students who need to travel out of town don't find this to be too much of a problem. The public bus system is a good resource, but with everything being within walking distance, students hardly use it. Take advantage of this though; walking to your destinations is a great way for students, or anyone, to explore the city. Whether you're walking, driving, riding or flying, Charleston has whatever type of transportation you need, however unlikely it is that you might use it.

The College Prowler™ Grade on

Transportation: B

A high grade for Transportation indicates that campus buses, public buses, cabs, and rental cars are readily-available and affordable. Other determining factors include proximity to an airport and the necessity of transportation.

Weather

The Lowdown On...
Weather

Average Temperature

Fall:	67 °F
Winter:	50 °F
Spring:	70 °F
Summer:	81 °F

Average Precipitation

Fall:	3.4 in.
Winter:	3.3 in.
Spring:	3.6 in.
Summer:	6.8 in.

Students Speak Out On...
Weather

> **"It's like heaven here. The sun's always shining, and it never gets cold. I love it."**

Q "The winters are mild, and I'm thankful for that, but **summer feels like hell** here. Every time I walk out the door I feel like I'm about to melt."

Q "It gets really hot here in the summertime, and **the humidity is almost unbearable.** Sometimes we have 100 percent humidity! Do you know what that does to your hair?"

Q "Winter here is like spring to most other people. We all get chilly when it's 65 degrees outside…**'better bundle up!** It dropped below seventy degrees!"

Q **"Air conditioning is absolutely essential here.** No, opening the windows of your house will not keep you cool."

Q "I can't say it's temperate, because **the summers are so intensely hot**. But the winters here are so completely bearable that it makes up for the sweltering heat."

Q **"The weather here is kind of unpredictable.** When spring comes, the temperature fluctuates between really hot and dry to really cold and wet, and everything in between. If you're not used to it, your sinuses will pay the price."

Q "Most people here are from the South already, so they're used to the heat. But the rest of us have to get adjusted to the humidity and heat. **At least the beach is right there,** so if you need to cool off, just go to Isle of Palms or something."

Q "I love the heat here! It brings out the **girls in tiny skirts!"**

Q **"You have no other option but to wear very little clothing here.** It's not a matter of style or appearance. If you value your life in the summer here, you will dress like a skank. I'm sorry, but that's the way it is."

Q **"Get used to 80 degree weather.** There are maybe two months out of the year when it's not really hot and humid outside."

The College Prowler Take On...
Weather

If you're a fan of blistering cold and snowstorms, then C of C is not for you. As in the rest of the Southeast, summers are hot and humid and winters are mild. With such a variety of students, coming from all different places, reactions to the weather tend to be mixed. But one thing is for sure: get ready to sweat! Many a student at the College of Charleston comes to the South because they hate northern winters, and the general populace is at peace with the unpredictable, yet constant, change of the seasons. But the change of climate has taken its toll on some students not originally from the South. They soon learn that humidity and hair do not make good friends and sinuses tend to suffer as well. The heat is another issue altogether. Some students love to step out into sunny weather that's at least 80 degrees, while others, typically not native to the region, feel that ten seconds outside can melt the human body like an ice cube. There is a plus side to the southern heat, though. All the girls wear short skirts!

If you're hoping for maybe a little bit of snow, the chances are slim. Records and school history show that the last time school was shut down due to weather was the mid-70s, when there was an inch of ice on the ground. But if you're looking for sun, they've got plenty of that to go around. Eventually those who are new to the South will get used to the heat, but until they do, there's no chance that the school will be shut down because of too much sun.

The College Prowler™ Grade on

Weather: B+

A high Weather grade designates that temperatures are mild and rarely reach extremes, that the campus tends to be sunny rather than rainy, and that weather is fairly consistent rather than unpredictable.

Report Card Summary

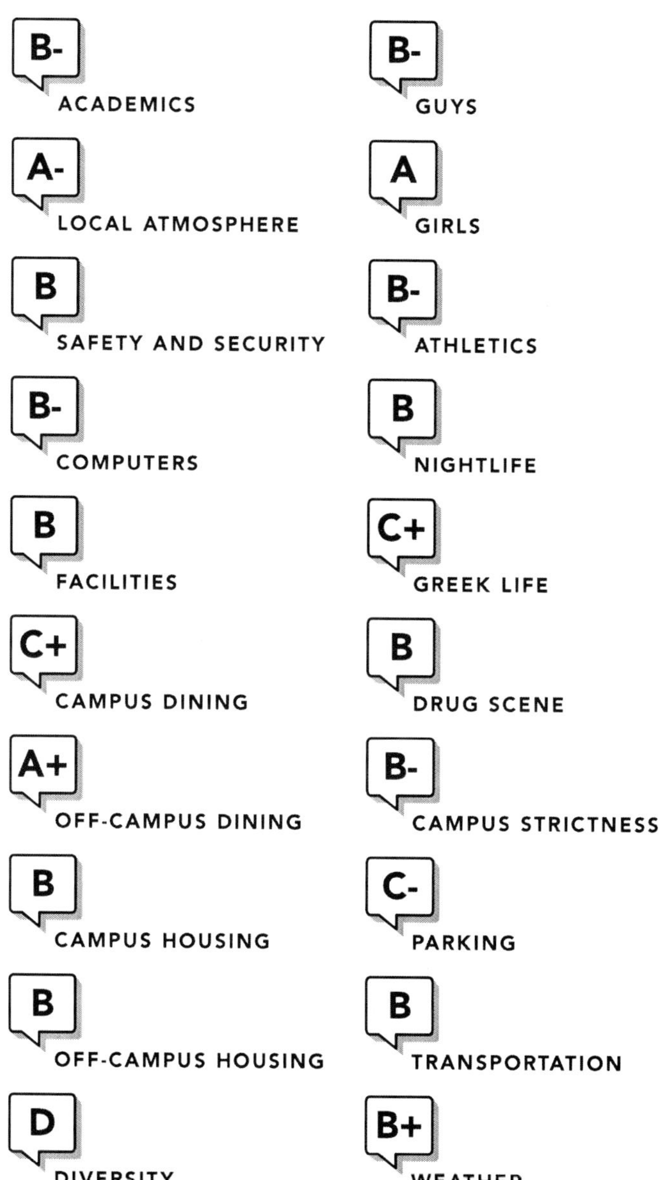

Overall Experience

Students Speak Out On...
Overall Experience

> **"I feel at home here, and I felt at home almost right away. Sometimes there are things about the city that I don't like, but the people and the atmosphere more than make up for that."**

Q "C of C doesn't have a reputation for much of anything. You're not getting the most exceptional education here; you're not participating in the craziest parties, or supporting the most successful teams. But **I wouldn't want to go anywhere else.** I feel like this is my home now."

Q "OK, **I only have one complaint, the heat!** But other than that Charleston is the greatest place I could have gone to college."

Q "I wanted to transfer my freshman year, but I decided not to, and I'm so glad I did! **I've made the greatest friends here,** and doors are really opening up for me with my education that I would have missed somewhere else."

Q "I met a lot of really unfriendly people when I first got here. I was thinking 'oh, Southern Hospitality will be nice,' and there wasn't any. **This isn't a typical Southern school.** It's about as metropolitan as you're going to get except for Atlanta."

Q "There are things that bother me about C of C, but that's not the school's fault. **I enjoy myself here,** and basically anyone can find their niche here."

Q **"Don't expect Charleston to be like Atlanta or New York.** It's not like any other city I've ever been in. It has its own charm, its own appeal, its own taste. If you're here for a while and you can't adjust to Charleston for what it is, then there's a good chance you won't enjoy your time at this school."

Q "I think that C of C can pretty much be the right place for anyone. **If you like to party a lot, come here.** If you don't like to party a lot, come here anyway. Charleston is not a place that can be described in one word. It's a combination of different things, just like the people who come here."

Q "The faculty is great, the school is great, the city is great. I know there are people here who aren't gaga over the atmosphere, or don't love their professors, or whatever. But for me, **I pretty much love everything about this place."**

Q "Sometimes I wish Charleston was bigger. **It's so laid-back and small-town like** as if it's not a small town at all. But I can tell you one thing, Charleston is unique, and so is the school."

Q "It's not a big place, so if you're looking for career opportunities, **you should use your time here to lead you to other cities and other places.** But I know people who have gotten really good jobs and have stayed in Charleston, and they're happy. Charleston does really help people branch out after graduation."

Q **"I love the feeling of this school** — it's just like Charleston — laid-back, relaxed, peaceful. It's so much better than going to a big university. You can really find yourself and be an individual here."

The College Prowler Take On...
Overall Experience

Most students acknowledge the fact that at the College of Charleston, they're experiencing something unique and rare. Not only is the city an interesting and fascinating place, but the years students will spend at C of C will be radically different than they would be at most other schools. Many schools are not located in the heart of a city as Charleston is, and many schools do not preserve the old while combining it with the new, the way the College of Charleston strives to. Although C of C may not have a well-known reputation for superior academics or sports, both the latter and the former are among the greatest in the nation, and many students come to care less and less about the acclaim that Charleston receives.

One cannot truly understand the appeal and rarity of attending the College of Charleston until they have been here a while, and though students do transfer out for various reasons (including simply not being happy as a C of C student), those who do remain here for all of their college years look back on their memories with nothing but contentment and pride. Charleston does its best to encourage its students and residents to enjoy the time they spend here, and students here will never be lacking in opportunity for their career or further education goals. Though it may be small and laid-back, the College of Charleston has many different qualities to be proud of and the students themselves have said that Charleston has become their home.

The Inside Scoop

The Lowdown On...
The Inside Scoop

Things I Wish I Knew Before Coming to C of C:

- The girls outnumber the guys almost 2 to 1

- The bricks on campus sidewalks are easy to trip on

- What was beyond downtown Charleston

- Be careful what meal plan you buy

- The acquired title of "Yankee" given to anyone from above the Mason-Dixon line

- How prevalent Greek Life is

- The number of Citadel jerks that hang out in the lobby of Barry dorm

- How unpredictable the weather can be

- More about public transportation

Tips to Succeed at C of C

- Have a general idea of what you want to major in

- Take classes you actually like

- Don't skip too many classes (even if they have no attendance policy)

- Be friendly with people in your classes

- Strive to make lasting friendships with the people you live with

- Check your e-mail every day

- Make an effort to communicate with your professors

- Learn to love the library

- Always dispute bad grades

C of C Urban Legends

- Joe E. Barry Dorm is rumored to be haunted by the ghosts of little girls that lived there more than 100 years ago when it was an orphanage, not a dorm.

- The cistern was once a popular place for fraternities to torment their pledges before it was filled with cement and turned into a grassy platform in front of Randolph Hall.

- Thirty years ago there was a war between Pi Kappa Alpha and Tau Kappa Alpha that apparently ended in both fraternities being kicked off campus.

School Spirit

With a basketball team of somewhat high reputation, students will rally behind C of C athletics even if they're not sports fans. Athletics at the College of Charleston are no more popular than theater, music or any other area of interest, and school spirit seems to be expended on all of these things. Musicians gather in the outdoor areas of campus and perform drum circles and students flock to see student-written and performed plays. The pride that students have in each other and in the College of Charleston reaches to all areas and goes far beyond athletics.

The Booze Cruise:

A popular event among students, the Booze Cruise is a boat party that occurs a couple times a month for students to basically get drunk and socialize while cruising around the battery.

Finding a Job or Internship

The Lowdown On...
Finding a Job or Internship

Firms that Most Frequently Hire Graduates:

PriceWaterhouse Coopers
Merrill Lynch
Bank of America
Sherwin Williams Co.
Blackbaud
Peace Corps
Charleston, Berkley amd Dorchester School Districts
Enterprise Rent-A-Car
Ferguson Enterprises

L.H. Robinson
Medical University of SC
Maersk Sealand
SPAWAR
Teach for America
Wachovia Bank
Automated Desk Trading

Graduates Who Enter Job Market Within One Year:

76%

If you are worried about finding a job after going to school, or if you are having a hard time making a decision for extended education, fear not. Career Services at the College of Charleston is there to help, and can assistant you in finding opportunities even before graduation.

Advice

Stay in touch with Career Services. As well as helping you with your long term goals, they can help you find part-time or full-time work both on and off campus while attending the College of Charleston.

Career Center Contact Information:

Lightsey Center

160 Calhoun St.

Lower Level, Room B-28

Phone: (843) 953-5692

E-mail: careersvs@cofc.edu

Website: http://www.cofc.edu/~career

To learn more about Career Services, check out their website. Here, you'll find links for parents, students, and alumni and information about internships, office hours, and more.

Resources and Services:

- On-campus and off-campus work
- Career counseling
- Placement advising
- Internships and work studies
- Graduate school advising
- CISTERNonline quick links for employment (long and short term)

The Lowdown On...
Alumni

Website:
http://www.cofc.edu/alumfami-
lyfriend/

Office:
18 Bull Street
Charleston, SC, 29424
E-mail: Alumni@cofc.edu
Phone: (843) 953-5630

Major Alumni Events

Events include parties to welcome alumni from areas all over the nation to local chapters in cities nationwide, picnics, Charleston Riverdogs' minor league baseball games, trips to various places such as San Francisco and Lake Tahoe.

Alumni Publications

"@ the Cistern" Online newsletter

Benefits Available

- Voting privileges at the annual meeting and service on one of various alumni association boards

- Reduced rates for receptions and events

- Access to campus facilities, including health centers, computer labs, Stern Center swimming pool, and the college library.

Student Organizations

Aikido club – http://www.cofc.edu/%7Eparent/aikiclub.htm

Alliance for Planet Earth

American Cancer Society

American Student Dental Association

Amnesty Internationa l – http://www.geocities.com/aicofc

Arabic Club

Association for Computing Machinery – http://www.cs.cofc.edu/%7Eacm

Aya Hwe M' - strives to provide a positive and enriching academic, social, spiritual and emotional college experience for African American Women.

Biology Club

Campus Outreach- helps college students grow successfully in their walk with Christ and thier leadership

Classics Club

Catholic Student Association (Compass)

Cougar Outdoor Recreation and Education (CORE)

Cougar TV - http://stu.cofc.edu/~tjbright/

Undergraduate Economics Council - http://www.econ.Charleston.edu/economicscouncil/

Undergraduate Film & Media Studies Council

Undergraduate History Council - http://www.Charleston.edu/college/HIS/undergrad/activities.html

Undergraduate Musicians' Council

Undergraduate Neuroscience Council - http://www.bcs.Charleston.edu/council/

Undergraduate Political Science Council - http://www.Charleston.edu/college/PSC/undergrad/news.php

English Club

Fencing

French Club

German Club - http://www.geocities.com/cofcgermanclub/

Geology Club

Golden Key

Gospel Choir

Habitat for Humanity

Historic Preservation Alliance (HPA)

Honors Program Student Association (HPSA) - http://www.cofc.edu/%7Ehpsa/

Indian Cultural Exchange

International Club - http://stu.cofc.edu/%7Ecofcic/

Jewish Student Union

Language and International Business Club

Lion's Club - http://www.geocities.com/cofclionsclub/Home.html

Marketing Club - http://stu.cofc.edu/%7Emktgclub/

Master of Environmental Studies Student Association (MESSA)

Miscellany - http://www.cofc.edu/Miscellany/

Muslim Students Association

National Organization for Reform of Marijuana Laws (NORMAL)

Philosophy Club

Physical Education Teacher Education Club (PETE)

Political Science Club - http://www.cofc.edu/%7Epolisci/

Portuguese Language Club

Presbyterian Student Association

Psychology Club - http://www.cofc.edu/%7Epsyclub/

Reformed University Fellowship - http://www.cofc.edu/RUF/

Russian Club - http://stu.cofc.edu/%7Ecofcic/

Shotokan Karate Club - http://www.cofc.edu/%7Eshotokan/

Sociology/Anthropology Club - http://www.cofc.edu/%7Esocyanth/club.htm

South Carolina Student Legislature

Spanish Club

Student Alumni Association - http://www.cofc.edu/~saa/

Student Government Association - http://www.cofc.edu/%7Esga/

Student Port - http://stu.cofc.edu/%7Estudport/index.htm

Student Science Society

Student Sports Medicine Association (SSMA) - http://www.cofc.edu/%7Erozzis/ssma.html

Student Union for Minority Affairs

Student Wellness Advisory Council

Ultimate Frisbee Organization

Visual Arts Club

Women's Rugby

Womyn's Forum

Young Democrats

Young Life

The Best & The Worst

The Ten BEST Things About C of C:

1	King Street
2	The Market
3	Beaches are close
4	The Waterfront
5	Marion Square
6	The Citadel
7	Greek Life
8	The Champ Card
9	Making bubbles in the fountain at Marion Square
10	College Lodge (It may be ratty, but its got charm!)

The Ten **WORST** Things About C of C:

1. The smell

2. The sidewalks on campus

3. The HomeZone's food

4. Not enough boys to go around

5. Some of the buildings have roaches or other critters

6. Guys from the Citadel

7. Greek Life

8. Public Safety

9. The overwhelming presence of Baptist churches

10. College Lodge

Visiting Charleston

The Lowdown On...
Visiting Charleston

Hotel Information

Andrew Pinckney Inn
Website: http://www.
andrewpinckneyinn.com
40 Pinckney St., Charleston
Phone: (843) 937-8800
Distance from Campus: Less
than 5 miles
Price Range: $80-$180

Best Western King's Inn
Website: http://www.
bestwestern.com
232 Meeting St., Charleston
Phone: (843) 723-7451
Distance from Campus: Less
than 2 miles
Price Range: $50-$100

Francis Marion Hotel
Website: http://www.
westinfm.com
145 Calhoun St., Charleston
Phone: (843) 722-0600
Distance from Campus: Less
than 1 mile
Price Range: $160-$190

John Rutledge House Inn
Website: http://www.
johnrutledgehouseinn.com/
116 Broad St., Charleston
Phone: (843) 723-7999
Distance from Campus: Less
than 5 miles
Price Range: $80-$180

→

Kings Courtyard Inn

Website: http://www.
kingscourtyardinn.com
198 King St., Charleston
Phone: (843) 723-7000
Distance from Campus: Less
than 3 miles
Price Range: $100-$200

The Meeting Street Inn

Website: http://www.
meetingstreetinn.com
173 Meeting St., Charleston
Phone: (843) 723-1882
Distance from Campus: Less
than 5 miles
Price Range: $80-$180

The Mills House Hotel

Website: http://www.
millshouse.com
115 Meeting St., Charleston
Phone: (843) 577-2400
Distance from Campus: Less
than 5 miles
Price Range: $90-$200

Planters Inn

Website: http://www.
plantersinn.com
112 North Market St.,
Charleston
(843) 722-2345
Distance from Campus: Less
than 5 miles
Price Range: $170-$675

Victoria House Inn

Website: http://www.
thevictoriahouseinn.com
205 King St., Charleston
Phone: (843) 720-2944
Distance from Campus: Less
than 3 miles
Price Range: $130-$200

Off the Peninsula:

Best Western Sweetgrass Inn

Website: http://www.
bestwestern.com
1540 Savannah Hwy.,
Charleston
Phone: (843) 571-6100
Distance from Campus: Less
than 10 miles
Price Range: $50-$100

Courtyard by Marriott

Website: http://marriot.com
35 Lockwood Drive,
Charleston
Phone: (843) 722-7229
Distance from Campus: Less
than 10 miles
Price Range: $90-$100

Holiday Inn Express
Website: http://www.
holidayinn.com
1925 Savannah Hwy.,
Charleston
Phone: (843) 402-8300
Distance from Campus: Less
than 10 miles
Price Range: $100-$150

Sleep Inn Charleston
Website: http://www.
sleepinn.com
1542 Savannah Hwy.,
Charleston
Phone: (843) 556-6959
Distance from Campus: Less
than 10 miles
Price Range: $50-$100

Take a Campus Virtual Tour

http://omt.cofc.edu/virtualtour/index.htm

Register for a tour at http://www.cofc.edu/admissions/
campus_visit.php or call admissions at (843) 953-5670.

The College also offers several open house sessions. For
information on upcoming open house sessions visit http://
www.cofc.edu/admissions/visiting/open_house.html. Or e-mail
openhouse@cofc.edu.

Directions to Campus

Driving from North:

- Get onto I-95 South
- Merge onto I-26
- Take exit 86A towards Charleston
- Merge onto US-171/Septima Clark EXWY
- Take exit 221A towards King Street/Savannah
- Follow King Street until intersection with Calhoun
- Turn right onto Calhoun Street
- Turn right onto St. Philip street
- Take left into St. Philip Garage

Directions from the West:

- Take I-26 East
- Merge onto US-17/Septima Clark EXWY via Exit 221A towards King Street/Savannah
- Follow King Street until intersection of with Calhoun
- Turn right onto Calhoun Street
- Turn right onto St. Philip Street
- Turn left into parking garage on St. Philip Street

Directions from South:

- Get onto I-95 North towards Savannah
- Merge onto US-17 N via exit 33 towards Charleston/Beaufort
- Take Lockwood Drive ramp
- Merge onto Lockwood Drive
- Turn slight left onto Calhoun ramp
- Turn right onto Calhoun Street
- Turn left onto St. Philip Street
- Turn left into St. Philip Street garage

Words to Know

Academic Probation – A student can receive this if they fail to keep up with their school's academic minimums. Those who are unable to improve their grades after receiving this warning can possibly face dismissal.

Beer Pong / Beirut – A drinking game with numerous cups of beer arranged in a particular pattern on each side of a table. The goal is to get a ping pong ball into one of the opponent's cups by throwing the ball or hitting it with a paddle. If the ball lands in a cup, the opponent is required to drink the beer.

Bid – An invitation from a fraternity or sorority to pledge their specific house.

Blue-Light Phone – Brightly-colored phone posts with a blue light bulb on top. These phones exist for security purposes and are located at various outside locations around most campuses. If a student has an emergency or is feeling endangered, they can pick up one of these phones (free of charge) to connect with campus police or an escort service.

Campus Police – Policemen who are specifically assigned to a given institution. Campus police are not regular city officers; they are employed by the university in a full-time capacity.

Club Sports – A level of sports that falls somewhere between varsity and intramural. If a student is unable to commit to a varsity team but has a lot of passion for athletics, a club sport could be a better, less intense option. If a club sport still requires too much commitment, intramurals often involve no traveling and a lot less time.

Cocaine – An illegal drug. Also known as "coke" or "blow," cocaine often resembles a white crystalline or powdery substance. It is highly addictive and dangerous.

Common Application – An application that students can use to apply to multiple schools.

Course Registration – The time when a student selects what courses they would like for the upcoming quarter or semester. Prior to registration, it is best to have an idea of several back-up courses in case a particular class becomes full. If a course is full, a student can place themselves on the waitlist, although this still does not guarantee entry.

Division Athletics – Athletics range from Division I to Division III. Division IA is the most competitive, while Division III is considered to be the least competitive.

Dorm – Short for dormitory, a dorm is an on-campus housing facility. Dorms can provide a range of options from suite-style rooms to more communal options that include shared bathrooms. Most first-year students live in dorms. Some upperclassmen who wish to stay on campus also choose this option.

Early Action – A way to apply to a school and get an early acceptance response without a binding commitment. This is a system that is becoming less and less available.

Early Decision – An option that students should use only if they are positive that a place is their dream school. If a student applies to a school using the early decision option and is admitted, they are required and bound to attend that university. Admission rates are usually higher with early decision students because the school knows that a student is making them their first choice.

Ecstasy – An illegal drug. Also known as "E" or "X," ecstasy looks like a pill and most resembles an aspirin. Considered a party drug, ecstasy is very dangerous and can be deadly.

Ethernet – An extremely fast internet connection that is usually available in most university-owned residence halls. To use an Ethernet connection properly, a student will need a network card and cable for their computer.

Fake ID – A counterfeit identification card that contains false information. Most commonly, students get fake IDs and change their birthdates so that they appear to be older than 21 (of legal drinking age). Even though it is illegal, many college students have fake IDs in hopes of purchasing alcohol or getting into bars.

Frosh – Slang for "freshmen."

Hazing – Initiation rituals that must be completed for membership into some fraternities or sororities. Numerous universities have outlawed hazing due to its degrading or dangerous requirements.

Sports (IMs) – A popular, and usually free, student activity where students create teams and compete against other groups for fun. These sports vary in competitiveness and can include a range of activities—everything from billiards to water polo. IM sports are a great way to meet people with similar interests.

Keg – Officially called a half barrel, a keg contains roughly 200 12-ounce servings of beer and is often found at college parties.

LSD – An illegal drug. Also known as acid, this hallucinogenic drug most commonly resembles a tab of paper.

Marijuana – An illegal drug. Also known as weed or pot; besides alcohol, marijuana is one of the most commonly-found drugs on campuses across the country.

Major –The focal point of a student's college studies; a specific topic that is studied for a degree. Examples of majors include physics, English, history, computer science, economics, business, and music. Many students decide on a specific major before arriving on campus, while others are simply "undecided" and figure it out later. Those who are extremely interested in two areas can also choose to double major.

Meal Block – The equivalent of one meal. Students on a "meal plan" usually receive a fixed number of meals per week.

Each meal, or "block," can be redeemed at the school's dining facilities in place of cash. More often than not, if a student fails to use their weekly allotment of meal blocks, they will be forfeited.

Minor – An additional focal point in a student's education. Often serving as a compliment or addition to a student's main area of focus, a minor has fewer requirements and prerequisites to fulfill than a major. Minors are not required for graduation from most schools; however some students who want to further explore many different interests choose to have both a major and a minor.

Mushrooms – An illegal drug. Also known as "shrooms," this drug looks like regular mushrooms but are extremely hallucinogenic.

Off-Campus Housing – Housing from a particular landlord or rental group that is not affiliated with the university. Depending on the college, off-campus housing can range from extremely popular to non-existent. Those students who choose to live off campus are typically given more freedom, but they also have to deal with things such as possible subletting scenarios, furniture, and bills. In addition to these factors, rental prices and distance often affect a student's decision to move off campus.

Office Hours – Time that teachers set aside for students who have questions about the coursework. Office hours are a good place for students to go over any problems and to show interest in the subject material.

Pledging – The time after a student has gone through rush, received a bid, and has chosen a particular fraternity or sorority they would like to join. Pledging usually lasts anywhere from one to two semesters. Once the pledging period is complete and a particular student has done everything that is required to become a member, they are considered a brother or sister. If a fraternity or a sorority would decide to "haze" a group of students, these initiation rituals would take place during the pledging period.

Private Institution – A school that does not use taxpayers dollars to help subsidize education costs. Private schools typically cost more than public schools and are usually smaller.

Prof – Slang for "professor."

Public Institution – A school that uses taxpayers dollars to help subsidize education costs. Public schools are often a good value for in-state residents and tend to be larger than most private colleges.

Quarter System (sometimes referred to as the Trimester System) – A type of academic calendar system. In this setup, students take classes for three academic periods. The first quarter usually starts in late September or early October and concludes right before Christmas. The second quarter usually starts around early to mid–January and finishes up around March or April. The last quarter, or "third quarter," usually starts in late March or early April and finishes up in late May or Mid-June. The fourth quarter is summer. The major difference between the quarter system and semester system is that students take more courses but with less coverage.

RA (Resident Assistant) – A student leader who is assigned to a particular floor in a dormitory in order to help to the other students who live there. A RA's duties include ensuring student safety and providing guidance or assistance wherever possible.

Recitation – An extension of a specific course; a "review" session of sorts. Because some classes are so large, recitations offer a setting with fewer students where students can ask questions and get help from professors or TAs in a more personalized environment. As a result, it is common for most large lecture classes to be supplemented with recitations.

Rolling Admissions – A form of admissions. Most commonly found at public institutions, schools with this type of policy continue to accept students throughout the year until their class sizes are met. For example, some schools begin accepting students as early as December and will continue to do so until April or May.

Room and Board – This is typically the combined cost of a university-owned room and a meal plan.

Room Draw/Housing Lottery – A common way to pick on-campus room assignments for the following year. If a student decides to remain in university-owned housing, they are assigned a unique number that, along with seniority, is used to choose their new rooms for the next year.

Rush – The period in which students can meet the brothers and sisters of a particular chapter and find out if a given fraternity or sorority is right for them. Rushing a fraternity or a sorority is not a requirement at any school. The goal of rush is to give students who are serious about pledging a feel for what to expect.

Semester System – The most common type of academic calendar system at college campuses. This setup typically includes two semesters in a given school year. The "fall" semester starts around the end of August or early September and finishes right before winter vacation. The "spring" semester usually starts in mid-January and ends around late April or May.

Student Center/Rec Center/Student Union – A common area on campus that often contains study areas, recreation facilities, and eateries. This building is often a good place to meet up with fellow students and is most commonly used as a hangout. Depending on the school, the student center can have a huge role or a non-existent role in campus life.

Student ID – A university-issued photo ID that serves as a student's key to many different functions within an institution. Some schools require students to show these cards in order to get into dorms, libraries, cafeterias, and other facilities. In addition to storing meal plan information, in some cases, a student ID can actually work as a debit card and allow students to purchase things from bookstores or local shops.

Suite – A type of dorm room. Unlike other places that have communal bathrooms that are shared by the entire floor, a suite has a private bathroom. Suite-style dorm rooms can house anywhere from two to ten students.

TA (Teacher's Assistant) – An undergraduate or grad student who helps in some manner with a specific course. In some cases, a TA will teach a class, assist a professor, grade assignments, or conduct office hours.

Undergraduate – A student who is in the process of studying for their Bachelor (college) degree.

ABOUT THE AUTHOR:

Before anything else is said, I want to express how thankful I
am to have been given this opportunity. This project has given
me insight into a field that I know for sure I want to be doing
for the rest of my life, and has helped me develop a beginner's
work ethic for writing that I know will only grow as time goes
on. I'm a junior at the College of Charleston pursing a major
in English and a double minor in creative writing, with an
emphasis in non-fiction and communications. This is more than
a first step for me, more than just an excuse to storm around
the house like a weathered professional screaming, "I'm up
against a deadline!" It has showed me what hard work really
can accomplish. I hope you enjoyed reading this book and
that it has given you a more honest and insightful glimpse into
C of C. If you have any questions or comments, please email
MelanieMurray@colleprowler.com.

Even though I was a crabby hermit locked in a room with
a computer for two months, I have many people to thank,
people who have helped in more ways than one: Mom and
Dad of course, Lauren, Nick, Becca, Sarah, Britt, Kathy, Jimmy,
Mamie, Bo, Lauren, Leah, Liz, and everyone at College
Prowler!

Melanie Murray

Notes

Notes

Notes

Notes

Notes

Notes

Notes

Notes

Notes

Notes

Notes

Notes

Notes

Notes

Notes

Notes

Notes

Notes

Need More Help?

Do you have more questions about this school? Can't find a certain statistic? College Prowler is here to help. We are the best source of college information on the planet. We have a network of thousands of students who can get the latest information on any school to you ASAP. E-mail us at *info@collegeprowler.com* with your college-related questions. It's like having an older sibling show you the ropes!

Email Us Your College-Related Questions!

Check out **www.collegeprowler.com** for more details.
1.800.290.2682

Notes

Tell Us What Life Is Really Like At Your School!

Have you ever wanted to let people know what your school is really like? Now's your chance to help millions of high school students choose the right school.

Let your voice be heard and win cash and prizes!

Check out **www.collegeprowler.com** for more info!

Notes

Do You Have What It Takes To Get Admitted?

The College Prowler Road to College Counseling Program is here. An admissions officer will review your candidacy at the school of your choice and create a 12+ page personal admission plan. We rate your credentials with the same criteria used by school admissions committees. We assess your strengths and weaknesses and create a plan of action that makes a difference.

Check out **www.collegeprowler.com** or call 1.800.290.2682 for complete details.

Notes

Pros and Cons

Still can't figure out if this is the right school for you?
You've already read through this in-depth guide; why not
list the pros and cons? It will really help with narrowing down
your decision and determining whether or not
this school is right for you.

Pros	Cons

Notes

Need Help Paying For School?

Apply for our Scholarship!

College Prowler awards thousands of dollars a year to students who compose the best essays. E-mail *scholarship@collegeprowler.com* for more information, or call 1.800.290.2682.

Apply now at **www.collegeprowler.com**

Notes

Get Paid To Rep Your City!
Make money for college!

Earn cash by telling your friends about College Prowler!

Excellent Pay + Incentives + Bonuses

Compete with reps across the nation for cash bonuses

Gain marketing and communication skills

Build your resume and gain work experience for future career opportunities

Flexible work hours; make your own schedule

Opportunities for advancement

Contact *sales@collegeprowler.com*
Apply now at **www.collegeprowler.com**

Notes

Do You Own A Website?

Would you like to be an affiliate of one of the fastest-growing companies in the publishing industry? Our web affiliates generate a significant income based on customers whom they refer to our website. Start making some cash now! Contact *sales@collegeprowler.com* for more information or call 1.800.290.2682

Apply now at **www.collegeprowler.com**

Notes

Reach A Market Of Over 24 Million People.

Advertising with College Prowler will provide you with an environment in which your message will be read and respected. Place your message in a College Prowler guidebook, and let us start bringing long-lasting customers to you. We deliver high-quality ads in color or black-and-white throughout our guidebooks.

Contact Joey Rahimi
joey@collegeprowler.com
412.697.1391
1.800.290.2682

Check out **www.collegeprowler.com** for more info.

Notes

Write For Us!
Get Published! Voice Your Opinion.

Writing a College Prowler guidebook is both fun and rewarding; our open-ended format allows your own creativity free reign. Our writers have been featured in national newspapers and have seen their names in bookstores across the country. Now is your chance to break into the publishing industry with one of the country's fastest-growing publishers!

Apply now at **www.collegeprowler.com**

Contact *editor@collegeprowler.com* or
call 1.800.290.2682 for more details.

Notes

Notes

Write For Us!
Get Published! Voice Your Opinion.

Writing a College Prowler guidebook is both fun and rewarding; our open-ended format allows your own creativity free reign. Our writers have been featured in national newspapers and have seen their names in bookstores across the country. Now is your chance to break into the publishing industry with one of the country's fastest-growing publishers!

Apply now at **www.collegeprowler.com**

Contact *editor@collegeprowler.com* or call 1.800.290.2682 for more details.

Reach A Market Of Over 24 Million People.

Advertising with College Prowler will provide you with an environment in which your message will be read and respected. Place your message in a College Prowler guidebook, and let us start bringing long-lasting customers to you. We deliver high-quality ads in color or black-and-white throughout our guidebooks.

Contact Joey Rahimi
joey@collegeprowler.com
412.697.1391
1.800.290.2682

Check out **www.collegeprowler.com** for more info.